The MKb 42, MP43, MP44 and the Sturmgewehr 44

© Copyright 2003

The MKb 42, MP43, MP44 and the Sturmgewehr 44
Propaganda Photo Series, Volume IV
by G. de Vries & B.J. Martens

ISBN 90-805583-6-2
Printed in China through Colorcraft Ltd., Hong Kong

Published by:
Special Interest Publicaties BV
P.O. Box 282
6800 AG Arnhem
The Netherlands

Fax: (+)31-26-4430824
E-mail: si@sipublicaties.nl
www.sipublicaties.nl

CONTENTS

An Infantry group prepares to cross a river or small lake with a so-called *Großer Floßsack* (large rubber dinghy). This boat could carry up to 2750 kilo, enough to transport an Infantry group of eight as in this picture, a mortar group, a motorcycle or a 37 mm anti-tank gun. The men are equipped with reversable camouflage uniforms. Among their small arms are an MG42 and an MP43/1.

Russia, February/March, 1944.

(Bundesarchiv Koblenz No. 693/290/20A)

PREFACE

The *Propaganda Photo Series*

The *Propaganda Photo Series* is a new series of books on World War II German small arms. Each volume covers all essential information on history and development, ammunition and accessories, codes and markings and contains photos of nearly every model and accessory.

The most important quality of the *Propaganda Photo Series*, however, is a unique selection of original German World War II propaganda photos. The combination of solid information and original photos makes the *Propaganda Photo Series* the most extensive and reliable source of German small arms "in-use", depicting weapons and their accessories as they were actually used.

The propaganda photos were collected from German and other archives, and were taken by official German war photographers. During World War II, there were about 2,500 official photographers and reporters, usually organized in special propaganda units covering all branches of the armed forces on all fronts. Their work was considered so important, that some of them were given permits that gave them immediate access to any form of transport at any time on any front.

The photographs were used by the Nazi press in Germany and the occupied countries to persuade the population of the Third Reich "point of view", as directed by the Ministry of Propaganda. Therefore, most of the original captions are very misleading or even flagrant lies, while the majority of the photos are posed. Some photos were found to be retouched to conceal the exact location or to add a Nazi symbol. On many occasions, extensive series of photos were shot, depicting the same soldier in different poses. Usually, the most warriorlike pictures were selected for publication.

Keeping these restrictions in mind, the photos nevertheless offer the most adequate information on the small arms as they were actually used. For this purpose they are published separately from the text and on a large format.

ACKNOWLEDGEMENTS

This book could not have been published without the assistance of the following institutions and individuals:

- Bundesamt für Wehrtechnik und Beschaffung, Wehrtechnische Studiensammlung (WTS), Koblenz, Germany: Dr. R. Wirtgen, Mr. H. Heinrich.
- Bundesarchiv Koblenz, Germany: Mrs. B. Kuhl.
- Bundesarchiv, Militärarchiv Freiburg, Germany.
- Military History Museum of Artillery, Engineering Troops and Signals, St. Petersburg, Russia: Colonel V.M. Krylov, Mr. A.N. Kulinsky.
- The former Ministry of Defence Pattern Room, Nottingham, United Kingdom: Mr. H. Woodend, Mr. R. Jones, Mr. J. Henshaw, Mr. N. Dixon, Mr. E. Rose, Mr. R. Sharrock, Mrs. C. Groves.
- Museum of Modern History, Ljubljana, Slovenia: Dr. D. Voncina, Mr. V. Martincic, Mrs. M. Kokalj Kocevar.
- Koninklijk Museum van het Leger en de Krijgsgeschiedenis, Brussels, Belgium: Mr. E. de Groote.
- Mr. J. Cross, Stoke on Trent, United Kingdom.
- Mr. T.B. Nelson, Alexandria, United States of America.
- Dr. G.L. Sturgess, Cambridge, United Kingdom.
- Mr. H.L. Visser, Wassenaar, The Netherlands.

PHOTO CREDITS

The pictures in this book were acquired from the following sources:

- Bundesamt für Wehrtechnik und Beschaffung, Wehrtechnische Studiensammlung, Koblenz, Germany.
- Bundesarchiv Koblenz, Germany.
- Bundesarchiv, Militärarchiv Freiburg, Germany.
- Military History Museum of Artillery, Engineering Troops and Signals, St. Petersburg, Russia.
- Russian Army Museum, Moskou, Russia.
- Finnish Arms Museum Foundation, Hyvinkää, Finland.
- The former Ministry of Defence Pattern Room, Nottingham, United Kingdom.
- Koninklijk Museum van het Leger en de Krijgsgeschiedenis, Brussels, Belgium.
- Museum of Modern History, Ljubljana, Slovenia.
- Nederlands Politiemuseum, Apeldoorn, The Netherlands.
- Mr. L. Erenfeicht, Warsaw, Poland.
- Mr. H.B. Lockhoven, Cologne, Germany.
- Mr. W. Odegaard, California, United States.
- Dr. G.L. Sturgess, Cambridge, United Kingdom.
- Mr. H.L. Visser, Wassenaar, The Netherlands.
- Mr. D.W. Zoetmulder, Leusden, The Netherlands.

INTRODUCTION

The Sturmgewehr

From its appearance, the *Sturmgewehr* 44 (assault rifle 44) and its predecessors are well-known. Their history, however, has long been shrouded in mystery and has sparked the imagination of writers, with sometimes dubious results. Although none less than Otto von Lossnitzer, technical director of the Mauser company, claimed on several occasions that the weapons were first used in the Winter of 1942/43, the first documented shipment to the front was in fact not made until April, 1943. Errors have been made concerning production figures of the MKb 42 (W) and (H) and the nomenclature of the different models, most generally concerning the MP43/1, which is often erroneously called the successor of the MP43, while in fact it was its predecessor. There is the famous, but often wrongly-told, story of how Hitler rejected the weapon and the existence of highly imaginative *Sturmgewehr* accessories, such as the curved barrel devices.

All this, however does not alter the historical importance of the *Sturmgewehr*. Its conception meant the introduction of a selective fire assault rifle, chambered for an "intermediate" cartridge. This concept was followed by almost all other nations after World War II and has survived until the present day.

The *Sturmgewehr* originated from the lessons learned by the Germans in World War I. Immediately following this war, many attempts were made to construct a new type of weapon, resulting in various remarkable designs. Finally, in the late 1930's, the company of C.H. Haenel in Suhl, and its chief designer and director Hugo Schmeisser, managed to produce a serviceable design. This was developed into the *Maschinenpistole* 43/1 in early 1943, and remained virtually unchanged – except for its designation – until the end of World War II.

Although it was introduced relatively late in the War, the *Sturmgewehr* was manufactured in considerable quantity. Some 424,000 pieces were made by a small number of major assembling companies, and innumerable sub-contractors. This was due to another important aspect of the *Sturmgewehr*: it could be produced in the simplest possible way, through the extensive use of stampings.

I WHAT'S IN A NAME?

The *Sturmgewehr* has the doubtful honour of being the most frequently renamed gun in history. The constant model re-designations have been the source of quite a lot of confusion, but fortunately, the available archive material can clarify most questions.

The prototype weapons were briefly referred to as *schwere Maschinepistole* (heavy submachine gun), before being rebaptised into *Maschinenkarabiner* (machine carbine). This was probably done to distinguish them from the regular *Maschinenpistole* (submachine gun) and *Maschinengewehr* (machine gun). As there were two models, one by Walther and one by Haenel, these were designated *Maschinenkarabiner* 42 (W) and 42 (H) respectively, although two known prototypes of the latter gun are marked M.K. 42 (H.S.). This abbreviation may refer to the designer, **H**ugo **S**chmeisser, to **H**aenel and **S**chmeisser, or to **H**aenel **S**uhl.

For unknown reasons, the weapons became again referred to as *Maschinenpistole* 43 by early 1943. By that time, the Walther design had vanished from the stage and the Haenel model had been improved from a weapon firing from an open bolt, to one firing from a closed bolt. These two versions were initially called MP43 A, being the MKb 42 (H), and MP43 B. This apparently gave rise to some confusion. Around August, 1943, the designations were changed again, this time to MP43/1 and MP43/2. The first was the model firing from a closed bolt, and the latter the original MKb 42 (H). The next step came when the design of the weapon was changed to mount the standard rifle grenade launcher. In its original form, the barrel was too thick to accept the standard K98k grenade launcher. A version with a stepped-down barrel was developed and this was simply referred to as MP43. Hence, the MP43/1 was not a successor to the MP43, but its predecessor.

In 1944 the designation was changed again. In April of that year, the MP43 was rebaptized to MP44. In October its name was changed again, this time into *Sturmgewehr* 44, as part of a larger project to introduce suggestive names for new types of weapons. In February, 1944, for example, Hitler had already approved names such as Panther, Tiger, Elefant, Goliath, Panzerschreck, Jagdtiger, Jagdpanther, Puppchen and Marder for heavier material. Although some authors state that the *Führer* himself invented the *Sturmgewehr* designation, the available material suggests the initiative was taken by Infantry general Jaschka. (1)

For the *Sturmgewehr* manufacturers, the frequent re-designations must have been a nightmare, as the weapon itself, the magazines and some accessories had to be marked accordingly. Again and again they had to change their dies. There may have been moments that nobody knew which was the correct designation and this led to weapons which were restamped, some even getting earlier or non-official designations. Such is the case with at least four known weapons, marked **M.P. 43 (H)**, in which that designation is crossed out by two machined lines and the new legend MKb 42 (H) neatly machined beside it.

In May, 1944, the army Infantry Department protested the constant changes of model designations because "thousands of working hours and many raw materials" were being wasted in the process. As described, the protest had little effect: some months later the MP44 became the *Sturmgewehr* 44.

Six different markings on *Sturmgewehr* variants. The top two are Haenel-made MKb 42's of which the one on the left initially got the non-existing designation M.P. 43 (H). The lower four weapons are basically similar, but due to constantly changing model designations, the markings had to be changed as well. (courtesy of Mundur I Bron Magazine Warsaw Poland, MoD Pattern Room, Brussels)

II HISTORY AND DEVELOPMENT

The birth of the *Sturmgewehr* was the final outcome of three lengthy, complicated and interrelated developments: the search for a semi-automatic rifle, the German desire for an *Einheitswaffe* (general purpose weapon) for the infantry, and the development of the so-called "intermediate" cartridge: a cartridge with a range and potential between pistol ammunition and full-power rifle and machine gun cartridges.

There were various reasons for the German interest in both a new weapon and an intermediate cartridge. During World War I, the Germans had discovered that the traditional role of the infantry rifle, the *Gewehr* 98, had been largely taken over by machine gun fire. The majority of the infantry fighting took place at distances of less than 400 meters. As the range of the 7.92 x 57 mm S-cartridge exceeded that distance by far, this led to the quite natural conclusion that the rifle cartridge was "overpowered".

The *Gewehr* 98 itself had several drawbacks as well, preventing a rapid and effective deployment at short distances. Both the rifle and its line of sight were too long, it took time and considerable strength to chamber a new round, and the magazine capacity of five cartridges was too small. Furthermore, the Great War had seen the introduction of new types of weapons, such as the semi-automatic rifle, the submachine gun and the light machine gun. By the end of the war, neither of these had reached their final stages of development.

The Germans had already started working on all these aspects for quite some time, as shown by the record of a meeting in June, 1921, between representatives of the Infantry Inspection, the Cavalry Inspection and the *Inspektion für Waffen und Gerät* (the Inspection for Weapons and Equipment).(2) The meeting, in the form of an informal discussion, mentions trials held earlier with a 6 mm cartridge, which were terminated due to extensive barrel corrosion. Without giving any details, the record also mentions experiments with caseless ammunition, and cartridges with aluminium cases (which in fact had been held in the 1890s). The latter had been discarded because the cartridges could not be stored for prolonged periods; the brass primer fell out of the aluminium case because of electrolysis.

The record explains that previous trials with self-loading rifles had not been succesful, due to the great recoil force of the S-cartridge. What was needed, most of those present agreed, was a weapon with a high rate of fire, a shorter cartridge, and an effective range up to 800 meters The whole was quite neatly summarized by *Oberstleutnant* von Dittelberger, who stated that the desire for "rapid automatic fire will lead to an improved submachine gun with better small-caliber ammunition".

The thoughts and suggestions of this meeting were further developed by the *Inspektion der Infanterie*, which produced a memorandum dealing with the desirability of a new type of weapon in January, 1923.(3) With considerable foresight, the Infantry Inspection laid down most characteristics of the later *Sturmgewehr*. It advocated the introduction of a smaller and lighter rifle, with semi- and full automatic firing capacity, a similar ballistic performance as the *Gewehr* 98 up to 400 meters, and a magazine capacity of 20 to 30 cartridges.

The development of such a weapon, the Inspection concluded, was closely linked to the ammunition it should fire. The 7.92 x 57 mm cartridge had several drawbacks which should, if possible, be corrected. When

This semi-automatic rifle was constructed in the 1920's by Rheinmetall-engineer Karl Heinemann. The gas-operated weapon has a gas choke at the muzzle end and a toggle-lock, in which the toggle opens to the right side. The serial number on the breech is 0. (St. Petersburg)

A semi-automatic rifle designed by armourer Hunneshagen of the *Inspektion für Waffen und Gerät* (the Inspection for Weapons and Equipment). From about 1924 onward, Hunneshagen developed at least two models of rifles and a light machine gun. The rifle pictured here, with locking flaps, has no serial number. It is marked S/Reichswehr eagle/35 on the buttplate. (St. Petersburg)

fired from weapons with a shorter barrel than the Gewehr 98 it produced a considerable muzzle flash, in moist air it created a lot of smoke, especially when fired from machine guns, and its recoil was considered quite heavy. As a result of all this, the *Inspektion für Waffen und Gerät* (IWG) was asked to contact the appropriate companies and designers to create such a new weapon.

Prototypes

During the 1920's and 30's, a great many designers and companies produced a steady range of prototypes, showing that the history of German self-loaders is far more complicated than has thus far been generally assumed. Some of these weapons chambered the standard 7.92 mm round, such as a semi-automatic rifles with locking flaps of one armourer Hunneshagen of the IWG, a toggle-lock design by Karl Heinemann of Rheinmetall, the weapons of Heinrich Freiherr von Wimmersperg, and several Mauser forerunners of the G35, such as the self-loading rifles 32, 33 and 34.

Others approached the matter from the cartridge point of view. By 1934, the Rheinisch-Westfälische Sprengstoff AG had developed an 8 x 46 and 7 x 46 mm cartridge, and DWM had made a 7 x 39.1 mm cartridge designated "Bergmannpatrone" for camouflage purposes. In 1935, Gustav Genschow came with a 7.75 x 39.5 mm cartridge. For the latter, Heinrich Vollmer developed a machine carbine, named M35, which was tried by the successor of the IWG, the *Heereswaffenamt*. Trials with both this weapon and cartridge lingered on until August, 1939, when both were quite suddenly rejected. The exact reasons for this are unknown. Some claim that the weapon was too expensive and complicated to make, being beautifully machined at a time when the army was already looking for simple means of mass production. Others suggest that the advent of war prompted the army to concentrate on those weapons which were in use and ready for full-scale production.

However this may be, there is one strange aspect to the history of the Vollmer M35/III, as the final model was known. At the time when weapon and cartridge were rejected, the orders for the development of exactly the same had been given to other companies. By 1938, the design of a new cartridge was commissioned from the Polte cartridge factory in Magdeburg, and a suitable weapon from the C.G. Haenel Waffen- und Fahrradfabrik in Suhl.(3)

The demands for the weapon were as follows:
– weight similar or less than the K98k
– length considerably shorter than the K98k
– precision and trajectory similar to the K98k up to 600 meters
– single-shot precision up to 400 meters
– possibility for automatic fire, with a firing rate between 360 and 450 rounds per minute
– possibility to use the existing rifle grenade launcher
– suitable protection from dust and dirt
– simple construction
– reliability in freezing cold and desert conditions

As the new cartridge took time to get its final shape, the construction of an appropriate weapon was delayed. In the course of 1939, Haenel-director Hugo Schmeisser made designs for a new locking system and in 1940, two prototype weapons were made to test the construction. These prototypes were made from machined parts. Once the basic elements of the new weapon had been established, the company Merz-Werke in Frankfurt developed a sheet metal receiver and the Würtembergische Metallwarenfabrik in Geislingen made the

Three different Mauser semi-automatic rifles. All three are fore-runners of the G35. From top to bottom, the weapons measure 125 cm (# 11), 120 cm (# 20) and 113 cm (# NVN) respectively. (St. Petersburg)

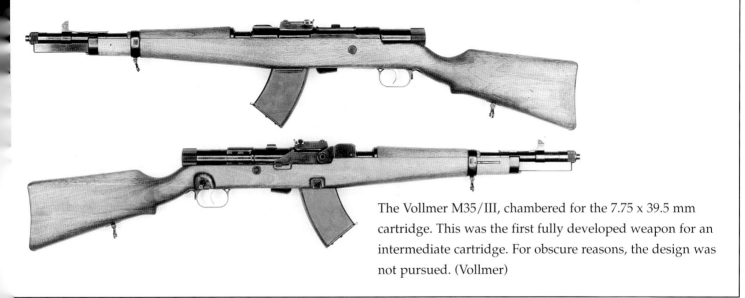

The Vollmer M35/III, chambered for the 7.75 x 39.5 mm cartridge. This was the first fully developed weapon for an intermediate cartridge. For obscure reasons, the design was not pursued. (Vollmer)

pistol grip. In the course of 1941, Haenel received an order for 50 of these weapons for trials.

Walther

In the meantime, the Waffenfabrik Walther in Zella-Mehlis had gotten word of the new project. Walther had been experimenting with self-loading carbines in the late 1930's and was, of course, quite interested. In January, 1941, the company got an order from the *Waffenamt* for the production of 200 pieces.

Walther was at a considerable disadvantage. Haenel had been working on its design for almost two years, while the Walther company had to start almost from scratch. It was not until early 1942 that the company had its first prototype ready. The gas-operating system consisted of an annular piston which surrounded the barrel and reciprocated within a cilindrical housing, similar to the earlier A-series of semi-automatic rifles. It has been debated whether Walther made the necessary stampings for these weapons itself or subcontracted these. The question cannot be completely answered here. One Walther gun, number 116, has the "awt" code of the Württembergische Metallwarenfabrik AG on the pistol grip, but another, number 0097, lacks this code.

On April 14, 1942, the two *Maschinenkarabiner* models were shown to Adolf Hitler. At the time, Haenel had made fifty prototypes while another fifty were in pre-paration. Walther had still finished only one specimen.

The *Führer* was not impressed. In his opinion, an infantry weapon should have a range of at least 1200 to 1500 meters. The troops needed sniper rifles and fast-firing machine guns, such as the recently introduced MG42, and not weapons for an intermediate cartridge.

Despite Hitler's disapproval of the weapons, 25 rifles of the Haenel model were sent to the Infantry School in Döberitz for evaluation in April, 1942. On June 30, the Infantry school presented its report.(4) Although the school had received 25 weapons, only thirteen serial numbers are mentioned. These are noted as 10, 11, 12, 13, 16, 21, 23, 26, 27, 28, 34, 35 and 45. The comments were as follows:

The original stock was shaped in a way that only the lower part could be pressed firmly to the shoulder. The Infantry School had designed a new stock, similar to that of the K98, which measured 26 cm, instead of 23.5 cm of the original one. The shape of this new stock was found satisfactory, but on the orders of the *Waffenamt* it was shortened to 23.5 cm again, to permit the future use of an optical sight.

The school found that the fire-selector should be positioned about 15 mm higher and the weapons should be equipped with a handguard. A model for this, which had been developed by WaPrüf 2, was too short and did not cover the gas cylinder and the gas chamber. The distance between the sights (40 cm) was found too short and the sights were positioned too high above the gas cylinder. The frame was considered too weak. The lanyard ring, which was attached to the gas cylinder, should be repositioned. The magazine loading tool was found impractical and superfluous, as the authorities wanted a possibility to load the magazine whilst in position.

As far as the magazine capacity was concerned, the Infantry School had tested types with a 10, 20, 25 and 30 round capacity. Only two options were considered viable: 25 and 30 rounds. The choice between the two depended on the height of the soldier. For those measuring 1.75 meters or more, a 30-round magazine was no problem, but for soldiers of smaller stature, the larger magazine presented problems while firing from a

These two pictures were taken in May or June 1942, during the trials of 25 Haenel-made *Maschinenkarabiner* by the Infantry School at Döberitz. The top picture shows the proposed magazine pouch. The lower gives a clear view of the trials weapon. Note the peculiar shape of the stock, and the lacking of both handguard and ejection port cover. (Militärarchiv Freiburg)

prone position. The Infantry School thus favoured the 25-round model, but WaPrüf had developed a 30-round model which measured 23,5 cm instead of 26 and thus solved the problem. To carry the magazines, the school had developed fabric pouches.

As a whole, the Infantry School considered the *Maschinenkarabiner* a desirable weapon from a tactical point of view. From a technical point, it still had some grave deficiencies. The parts of these trial models were not interchangeable, and as the weapons fired from an open bolt, they lacked precision at distances from about 600 meter onward. Precision was further deteriorated by the short barrel and short sight line.

In November, 1942, the chief of the Waffenamt published a memorandum about the *Maschinenkarabiner*, stating the desired qualities of weapons and cartridge.(5) The memorandum showed pictures of the MKb 42 (W), the G41, a prototype G43, the recently developed *Fallschirm-jägergewehr* 42 and an improved Haenel weapon. The latter, referred to as MKb 42 (H) *aufschießend,* or MP43 B, with serial number 02, was a new version, modified to fire from a closed bolt. According to the *Waffenamt*, only one of these new models had been produced, a further three being expected in December.

The Mkb 42 (H) *aufschießend* had a new type of stock, the sights had been lowered and it was equipped with a sheet-metal handguard. Such a weapon was demonstrated in November, 1942, to the General Staff, which was very pleased with it. Adoption of the *Maschinenkarabiner* would increase fire-power, the guns were easy to produce (the *Waffenamt* estimated an output of 25,000 per month by September, 1943), the new type of cartridge would save on pistol ammunition and finally, the Germans could not afford to lag behind any longer on the Soviet Simonov and Tokarev semi-automatic rifles

and the U.S. Garand. As a result of all this, the General Staff proposed a large-scale troop trial, resulting in a decision for adoption that same winter.

In taking this decision, however, the Germans posed themselves several problems. First and foremost, Hitler continually refused to recognise the advantages of the *Maschinenkarabiner*. In November, 1942, he had the chief of the Army inform all parties involved that his soldiers needed self-loading rifles and submachine guns, instead of a general purpose gun with a new type of ammunition.

To decide which type of self-loading rifle was most suitable, Hitler ordered practical trials with three models developed by the Gustloff-Werke in Suhl (the former company of Simson & Co), designated 206/3, 206/4 and 208. The development of these weapons, chambering the standard 7.92 mm round and being able to fire fully automatic, had been officially ordered in July, 1942. The army, however, had its own ideas.

Early in December, 1942, the *Maschinenkarabiner* and a prototype of the Gustloff 206 were demonstrated to high Army officials. That same month, the Infantry School conducted a series of practical trials with the K98k, the MKb 42 (H) *aufschießend* and the Walther model, of which the first series had been finished shortly before.(5) The Infantry School clearly favoured the Haenel design, for its robust construction, easy disassembly and longer line of sight. It noted only minor deficiencies, such as a loose handguard and the fact that the ejection port cover pushed the rear sight slightly upwards when the latter was set at distances of 200 or 300 meters. The Walther design was, in the eyes of the Infantry School, extremely complicated and sensitive. Under normal conditions, the gas piston rapidly jammed. It could be expected that a small amount of dirt or sand, or a slight denting of the

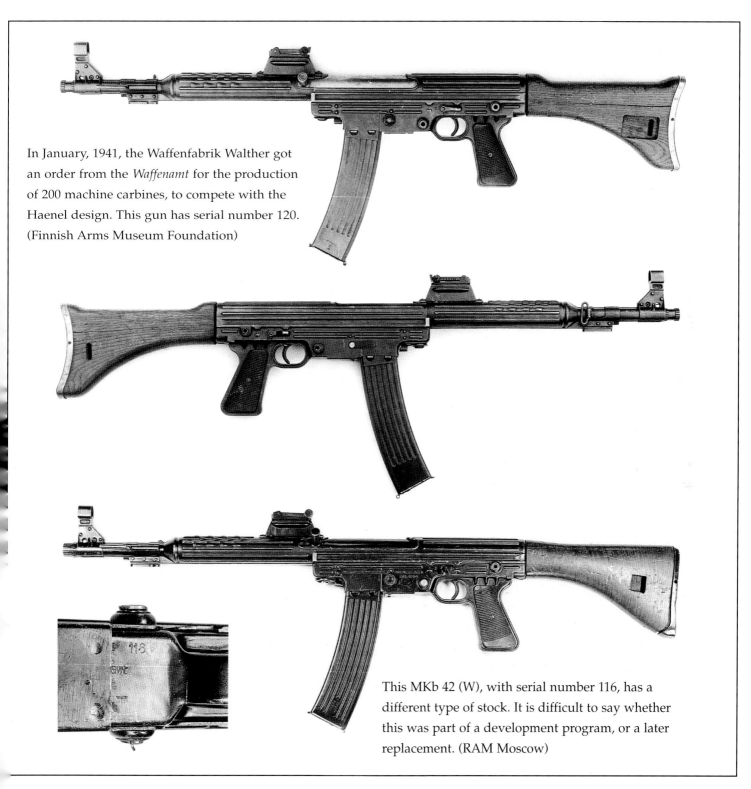

In January, 1941, the Waffenfabrik Walther got an order from the *Waffenamt* for the production of 200 machine carbines, to compete with the Haenel design. This gun has serial number 120. (Finnish Arms Museum Foundation)

This MKb 42 (W), with serial number 116, has a different type of stock. It is difficult to say whether this was part of a development program, or a later replacement. (RAM Moscow)

sheet metal piston jacket, would block the movement of the piston, thus rendering the weapon useless. (6) The favourable report on the MKb 42 (H) clearly shows that weapon had been greatly improved. At the same time it meant the end of the Walther design. As far as the Haenel weapon was concerned, the Infantry School judged that, once the noted deficiencies had been removed, it would give equal precision to the K98 for distances up to 500 meters.

The army by now considered the development of the MKb 42 (H) nearly completed. But there were still some problems. In the course of 1942, the Luftwaffe had ordered the development of a *Maschinenkarabiner* of its own. This *Fallschirmjägergewehr* fired the standard rifle cartridge. As the army was interested in a uniform armament, it proposed competitive troop trials with both the FG42 and the MKb 42. This proved impossible, as the FG42 faced serious production problems.

In January, 1943, the *Waffenamt* listed the various possibilities. The development of the semi-automatic G43 was finished and this weapon could go into production. The FG42 was still in the development phase. The same went for the Gustloff 206. Mass production of this weapon could only begin 12 to 18 months after its development had terminated. Of the improved MKb 42 (H), for unknown reasons now renamed *Maschinepistole 43*, 15 pieces were tested by the Waffenamt and mass production could begin by mid-1943.

Thus, the MP43 was the only new fully automatic Infantry weapon ready for production. The general staff tried once more to get Hitler's approval of the new weapon. On February 6, 1943, the *Führer* was demonstrated the improved MKb 42 (H), but once again he declined.(7) The MKb should not be produced and all work on the project should be halted. At the same time,

Hitler again demonstrated his preference for semi-automatic rifles, deciding upon the adoption of the G43 and continuation of the development of the Gustloff 206. Hitler's renewed and explicit ban on the MKb had little effect on the planned troop trials. In February, 1943, the *General der Infanterie* sent in a plan for these trials. A total of 1500 MKb's were to be sent to six divisions of *Heeresgruppe Nord*. A production plan, drawn up in March, specified that 9000 MKb 42s were to be made from April to June 1943, while mass production of the improved MP43 would begin in July.

These decisions are somewhat of a mystery. Why did the German army order the production of larger numbers of the earlier version of the MKb 42, firing from an open bolt, when tests had showed the superiority of the improved design, firing from a closed bolt? The reasons for this are unknown, but on April 10, 1943, the Army High Command informed *Heeresgruppe Nord* that 2000 MKb's had been sent, this being the first documented shipment ever made to the front.(8) Included in this batch were 2 or 3 handmade MP43's. As larger quantities of the latter model would become available, they would be sent to the front as well. Only when sufficient quantities of the MP43 became available, could the troop trials begin.

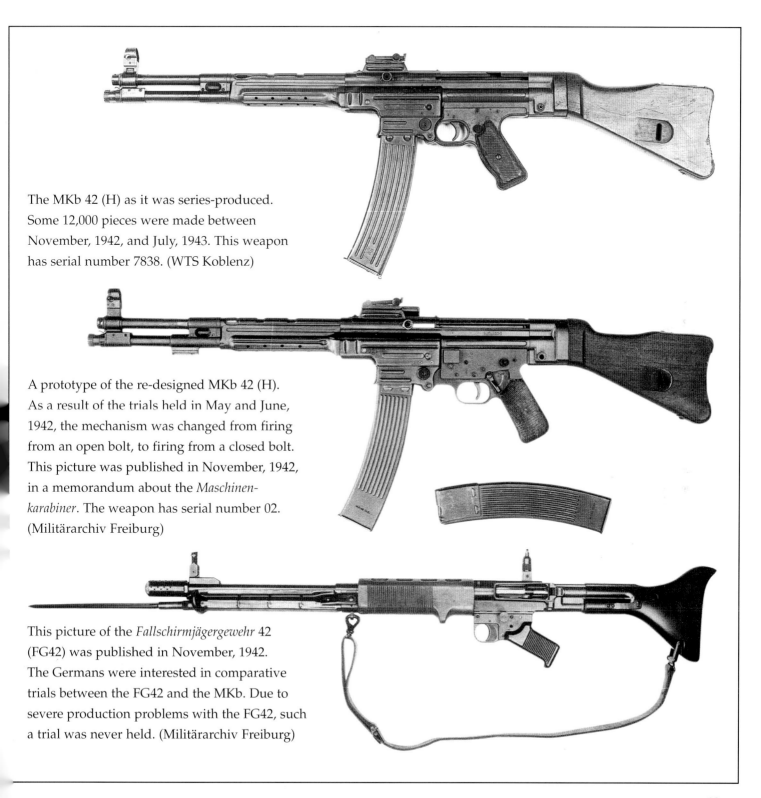

The MKb 42 (H) as it was series-produced. Some 12,000 pieces were made between November, 1942, and July, 1943. This weapon has serial number 7838. (WTS Koblenz)

A prototype of the re-designed MKb 42 (H). As a result of the trials held in May and June, 1942, the mechanism was changed from firing from an open bolt, to firing from a closed bolt. This picture was published in November, 1942, in a memorandum about the *Maschinenkarabiner*. The weapon has serial number 02. (Militärarchiv Freiburg)

This picture of the *Fallschirmjägergewehr* 42 (FG42) was published in November, 1942. The Germans were interested in comparative trials between the FG42 and the MKb. Due to severe production problems with the FG42, such a trial was never held. (Militärarchiv Freiburg)

III TRIALS AND ADOPTION

By April, 1943, the MP43 B (in most correspondence simply referred to as MP43) had been developed to the extent that larger quantities were to be sent to the front for extended troop trials. These plans were initially hampered, however, by production problems. The modification of the weapon from an open-bolt into a closed-bolt design meant several drastic changes, among others in the construction of the grip assembly. In March, 1943, MP43 production was scheduled to be 1,000 in June, 4,000 in July and 6,000 per month onward. In reality, only about 2,000 guns were made between June and September, due to *"Anlaufschwierigkeiten beim Griffstuck 43"* (initial problems with the grip unit 43).

Hitler's approval

By September, 1943, all parties involved had come to the conclusion that the MP43 would have to be officially adopted for general Infantry use. The *General der Infanterie von der Organisationsabteilung*, for instance, advocated immediate mass-production of the weapon, for several reasons. At the time, the German troops on the Eastern front were using some 13,500 Soviet submachine guns, 18,000 captured machine guns and some 202,000 Soviet rifles, which needed urgent replacement. Furthermore, the Soviets themselves were using rapidly increasing numbers of submachine guns, to which the MP43 would be an appropriate answer.

Still, there were some major problems to solve. First of all, there was a serious ammunition shortage. In May, 1943, there was a reserve of 12 million *Kurzpatronen*. Production was estimated to reach four million in May and five million per month from June onward. This may seem impressive, but it was very little compared to the 220 million rifle cartridges which were manufactured per month. As each MP43 was estimated to have a monthly expenditure of 6,000 rounds, it meant that by October, only about 6800 weapons could be fully equipped with ammunition. The bottleneck, therefore, lay not so much in the production of the weapons, but in that of the cartridges and this would continue to be the case throughout the war.

Then there was another matter. Although weapons were produced and shipped to the front, Hitler had explicitly banned development of the MP on several occasions. His approval was of the utmost importance for any further action. Karl Otto Saur, head of the technical department of the *Reichsministerium für Bewaffnung und Munition*, took on the job to persuade the *Führer* once more. Saur visited Hitler at his headquarters on September 30, and October 1, 1943. His mission was successful, partly due to favourable front reports, and partly by holding up the prospect of fantastic production numbers: ultimately, there should be three to four million MP's and some eight billion cartridges. As the result of the meeting, Hitler finally changed his mind. He commanded an initial production of 30,000 MP43's per month to replace the MP38 and 40, and at the same time ordered the production of the latter weapons to be halted.(9)

The Infantry Program

This decision was somewhat premature, for the MP38 and 40 could not yet be retired. It did, however, permit the authorities to extend the planned troop trial to other army groups. At the same time, Hitler's decision initiated the thoughts on what the German armed forces really needed. In November, 1943, *Oberstleutnant* Inhofer from

An MKb 42 (H) shown from the right side and field-stripped. This particular weapon, with serial number 5804 is equipped with a bayonet lug. None of the trial reports, however, mentions the use of a bayonet. (WTS Koblenz)

the *Heereswaffenamt*, produced a memorandum about the desirability to introduce a so-called Infantry Program.(10) He advocated a *"reinrassige Bewaffnung der Infanterie-Kompanie"* (pure-blooded armament of the infantry company). According to Inhofer, there were far too many different types of special weapons and ammunitions. His memorandum gradually climbed through the hierachy, until it reached the highest levels by the end of the year.

Inhofer's ideas would ultimately result in the establishment of the *Sonderkommission Infanteriewaffen* (special committee on infantry weapons) in July, 1944, whose extended activities will be discussed in Chapter V. In early 1944 the effect was limited to a specification of production goals for the coming year. A meeting at Speer's ministry on January 14, 1944, decided on monthly production of 100,000 MP43s with 200,000,000 cartridges. In the proceedings it was duly noted, however, that this was a goal, not a promise.

Quite rightly so, because the figure contrasted sharply with reality. In February, 1944, the Army High Command noted that the production of both weapons and ammunition was only a fraction of the planned amount, due to a lack of raw materials and Allied bombings.(11) Up to that month, only some 22,900 MP43/1 and MP43 had been made, the production of the MP43/1 being halted in December in favour of the MP43. Less than half had actually been distributed: 358 to *Heeresgruppe A*, 749 to *Heeresgruppe Süd*, 3732 to *Heeresgruppe Mitte*, 4438 to *Heeresgruppe Nord* and 41 to *Heeresgruppe D*, making a grand total of 9318 weapons.

Apart from the general shortage of arms and ammunition there was another matter. While Hitler had envisaged the MP43 to replace the MP38 and 40, the Army High Command wanted it to replace the K98k as well, thus effectively making it a general purpose weapon for the infantry. In January, 1944, Hitler agreed to a troops trial which had to decide whether this replacement was desirable. The 1st Infantry Division of *Heeresgruppe Süd* and the 32nd Infantry Division of *Heeresgruppe Nord* were destined to form units which should be armed with the MP43 exclusively. In late April, 1500 more weapons had reached the front. Meanwhile, the weapon had both been officially adopted and re-baptized again. The exact date of adoption is unclear. On March 16, Wa Prüf 2 Ib wrote to the General Headquarters that the MP43 was considered ready for adoption and purchase; on April 25, the General Staff wrote that, in order to make a clear distinction of the newly adopted firearms, the MP43 had received the final designation of MP44.(12)

In June, 1944 the situation was such that the 1st Infantry Division could be equipped with the MP44. A full replacement of the K98k, however, was not possible. Since the problems with a rifle grenade launcher and a suitable telescopic sight had not yet been solved, the troops had to retain some K98's for these purposes. The division handed in its report in September. The troops had judged the MP44 an excellent general purpose weapon, with only minor deficiencies, such as the rather weak springs of the magazine bottom piece and the dust cover. Some units had found the hole in the stock for the mainspring to be too narrow, as a result of which the spring was squeezed.

All these mishaps could easily be corrected, but still there was one major problem: insufficient ammunition. This was clearly described in a letter of the Army High Command from June 16, 1944, in which it said: "In the event that future ammunition supply will permit a corresponding equipment, the MP44 is destined to become the general purpose weapon of the Infantry".(13).

An MKb 42 without bayonet lug. Apart from this lug, all Haenel-made MKb's are similar. About 12,000 of these weapons were made and some remained in use up to the end of World War II. This weapon has serial number 7838. (WTS Koblenz)

When the MKb 42 had been redesigned to fire from a closed bolt, it got the designation MP43 B, and later MP43/1. About 14,000 pieces of this model were made, which are readily recognisable by the unstepped barrel and the square front sight pedestal. This weapon has serial number 2554a and was made in 1943. (WTS Koblenz)

In late 1943, the design of the MP43/1 was slightly modified so that it could be equipped with the standard rifle grenade launcher, the *Gewehrgranatgerät* 42. The front part of the barrel of this MP43 was stepped down and the front sight pedestal was redesigned. This weapon has serial number 8904 and was made in 1944. (WTS Koblenz)

In April, 1944, the MP43 was rebaptised into MP44. This particular weapon is a very late production version which has some simplifications of the housing, just above the magazine opening. The serial number is 26G and the weapon was made in 1945. (WTS Koblenz)

In October, 1944, the MP44 was rebaptised again, this time into *Sturmgewehr* 44. The disassembled weapon (serial number 6016af/45) is similar to the MP44. The one on top features some slight modifications, such as the omission of the threaded muzzle end, which resulted in a simplified front sight. This weapon has the somewhat remarkable number 00-30. (Brussels and Finnish Arms Museum Foundation)

IV MODIFICATIONS

From its first demonstration in early 1942, to the end of World War II, the *Maschinenkarabiner* underwent several modifications. The initial trials and the change from an open-bolt into a closed-bolt weapon have been discussed earlier. The late war-time experiments will be treated in the next chapter. Here, the focus will be on the production guns.

The only notable difference between the series-made MKb 42 (H) is that some of them have a bayonet lug and some do not. The reason for this is not quite clear. None of the trial reports mentions the use of a bayonet. It has been speculated that the *Seitengewehr* 42 (SG42, a combination of a bayonet, field knife and multi-purpose tool) was especially developed for the MKb, but no documentary evidence has been found to support or reject this hypothesis. If it were true, the idea was soon dismissed. From the MP43/1 onward, the bayonet lug was dropped, while the SG42 continued to be developed. The MP43/1 differed from the MKb 42 (H) mainly through its closed bolt mechanism, a shortened gas plug, and a redesigned front sight and pistol grip housing with a safety catch on the left side, above which the fire selector switch was positioned; features which were already present on the MKb42 (H) *aufschießend*.

As the MP 43/1 was supposed to be a general purpose weapon, it was investigated if it could be equipped with a rifle grenade launcher. Some experiments seem to have been conducted with a screw-on launcher, but it was far more logical to use the launcher of the K98k, the *Gewehrgranatgerät 42*. This proved impossible, due to the thickness of the MP's barrel. A slightly modified version, called MP43, got a stepped-down barrel and a redesigned front sight pedestal so that the standard grenade launcher could be mounted, albeit that the muzzle nut had to be removed.

In December, 1943, representatives of the *Waffenamt* and the Haenel factory discussed the final configuration of the MP43.(14) Some small amendments were made. It was decided to harden the takedown tool, used to unscrew the gas vent plug, and to provide it with a circular groove at its end. This way, the tool could be hooked inside one of the holes of the handguard, making this easier to remove. A wooden handguard was considered superfluous and, although not specifically mentioned in the proceedings of the meeting, the mounting rails for the ZF41 disappeared from the sides of the rear sight.

Furthermore, it was suggested to discard the thread and nut on the muzzle, which served as an attachment for a blank firing device. In 2 thought such a device was superfluous in wartime while the omission meant a simplification in production – besides, blanks were never made in sizeable quantity. For the moment, however, the threaded muzzle end was retained, as there were plans to equip the MP with a silencer. Nothing came of this, so the barrel nut and thread were discarded in the summer of 1944. At the same time, the mounting for the front sight was simplified.

Magazines

At the end of 1943, the Infantry Department advocated the construction of a magazine in which the follower caught the bolt once the last shot had been fired.

Two samples were favourably tested. In January, 1944, the *Heerewaffenamt* agreed to adoption, but it seems that production did not get under way before the war ended.

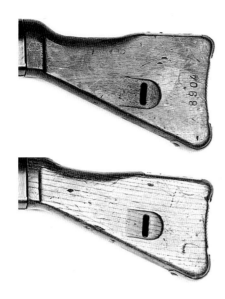

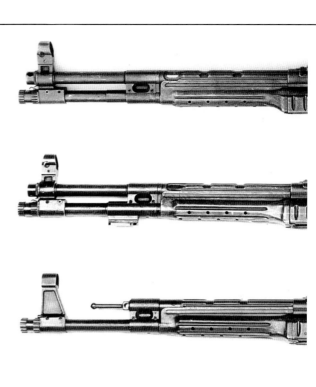

From Mid-1944 onward, the *Sturmgewehr* got a modified stock of somewhat smaller dimensions, which fitted the rifle holders in vehicles. Shown here are the old (top) and the new type of stock (bottom). (WTS Koblenz)

All MKb 42's and the majority of the MP43/1 were equipped with mounting rails for a telescopic sight on the rear sight pedestal. This was done in anticipation of the adoption of a telescope, but although several trials were held, such an adoption never occurred. (RAM Moscow)

The easiest way to distinguish between the different varieties of the *Maschinenkarabiner* is to look at the muzzle end. From top to bottom: MKb 42 (H) without bayonet lug, MKb 42 (H) with bayonet lug, MP43/1 (straight barrel and square front sight pedestal), MP43 and 44 (stepped barrel), and late-production StG 44 (no muzzle thread and simplified front sight pedestal). (WTS Koblenz)

The same went for a newly developed 25-round magazine in early 1945. Following complaints from the troops that the magazine spring went lame when the magazine was loaded to its full 30-round capacity, it was ordered to load only 25 cartridges. To facilitate this, the army staff wanted an opening in the magazine housing, covered by celluloid. This idea was rejected because it would complicate manufacture, but tests were held with other kinds of markers. In March, 1945, the Infantry School finally proposed a magazine follower with an elongated bottom which would be stopped by the magazine bottom plate once 25 cartridges had been loaded.(15) Although a 25-round magazine was included in a listing of accessories of that same month, it seems unlikely that any were made.

Rear sight

In 1943, In 2 asked for a redesign of the rear sight. Instead of a 100 meters increments, it was to get a 50 meters-increments graduation, and the possiblity of placing the leaf upright to act as a sight for rifle grenades. Three prototype sights were made, but the project was not pursued because the attention soon focused on a separate rifle grenade sight. In July, 1944, the *Waffenamt* again advocated a 50 meter graduation, ranging up to 400 meters instead of 800. The proposal was cancelled in November of that same year, but it may be possible that some sight leaves with 50 meters increments graduation were made, for this change was included in a reprint of the *Sturmgewehr* manual of December, 1944.

Stock and bolt

One of the changes that was actually implemented, concerned the stock. The MP43 had the stock that had been developed by WaPrüf 2. Once the weapons became more widely distributed, it transpired that this stock did not fit the vehicle holders. In March, 1944 a small trial was held with two MP43's with a redesigned stock which, at its rear part, had the dimensions of the K98k stock. The Infantry School was ordered to see if these stocks fitted the rifle holders and if they affected the performance of the weapon. The test had a favourable result and so the new type of stock was introduced by mid-1944. Another small modification concerned the bolt. From mid-1944 onward this got a groove next to the extractor, to prevent the latter from jamming due to the remains of lacquer from the steel cartridge cases.

Fire selector

A final proposition that was never pursued, was to block the fire selector. In early 1945, several units complained that insufficiently trained troops tended to fire their weapon fully automatic only. The proposal was denied, because it would severely impede the performance of the weapon.

Finally, it should be noted that the changes that were actually implemented can be dated only roughly. At the time a decision for modification was made, new drawings had to be prepared and distributed to as many as a few dozen sub-contractors. The assembling companies may have had vast stocks of the earlier parts which were used up first. The best illustration for this is the existence of receivers marked MP44, made in 1945 – at least three months after the weapon had been designated *Sturmgewehr 44*.

Two different versions of the bolt. From mid-1944 onward, the bolt got a groove next to the extractor, to prevent it from jamming through remainders of lacquer of the steel cartridge cases. (Brussels)

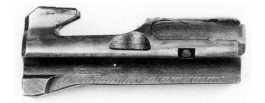

By the end of the war, the German army became more and more "de-motorised" through vast losses of material. Some units were equipped with bicycles and this picture shows a proposition to transport both an MP43/1 and a mine. (Militärarchiv Freiburg)

V STURMGEWEHR EXPERIMENTS

In the Summer of 1944, the Germans established a *Sonderkommission Infanteriewaffen* (special committee on infantry weapons). The first meeting of this committee was held on July 14 and 15, 1944, at the *Reichsministerium für Rüstung und Kriegsproduktion*, Pariser Platz 4, Berlin. The meeting was headed by *Wehrwirtschaftsführer* Otto von Lossnitzer (also technical director of the Mauser company) and had an impressive attendence list. The committee consisted of several permanent members, such as the manufacturer Fritz Walther, and a number of working groups. The working group for pistols, flare pistols and rifles was headed by chief engineer Karl Barnitzke from Gustloff-Werke in Suhl, the submachine working group by Haenel-director Hugo Schmeisser and the machine gun working group by Dr. Ing. Wilhelm Gruner from Großfuss. The committee had far-reaching authorities. Its decisions could only be revoked by minister Speer or Hitler himself.

The purpose of the committee was to list all ongoing development projects, to stimulate those which were deemed necessary, and to cancel those which were not *"Kriegsentscheidend"* (war decisive). A list of 187 projects was included with the invitation. A full description is far beyond the scope of this book, but some of the more interesting ones should be mentioned here:

A 7.65 mm Gustloff Pistol, a simplified Mauser HSc, a Mauser 9 mm pistol with tilting barrel, a sheet-metal P38, a 9 mm revolver by Mauser, Deutsche Werke and the Böhmische Waffenfabrik, emergency flare pistols by Walther, DWM and Appel, the Gustloff selfloading rifles 206 and 208, Mauser selfloading rifles 03 and 07, the infantry rifle G42 (B) by the Waffenwerke Brünn, a fully automatic G43 by Walther, a G43 (G) from pressed steel by Gustloff, several experimental MG42s, and an MG43. As far as the MP44 and similar weapons were concerned, the development projects were the following: (16)

Project	Company	Status
MP44 for the 9 mm *Patrone 08*	Erma	Halted
Simplified MP44	Erma	Production problems
Simplified MP44	Haenel	Ten pieces under troop trial
Retarded blow-back MP	Mauser	Design finished
Roller-locked MP 43	Mauser	Weapon test-fired
MP SS 44	Brünn	Six weapons ready, project interrupted
Blow-back MP 507	Gustloff	Third model under development
Blow-back MP 508	Gustloff	Second weapon under construction
Retarded blow-back MP	Großfuß	Two weapons under construction
Double-barreled MP, 7.92 mm	Brünn	Project abandoned

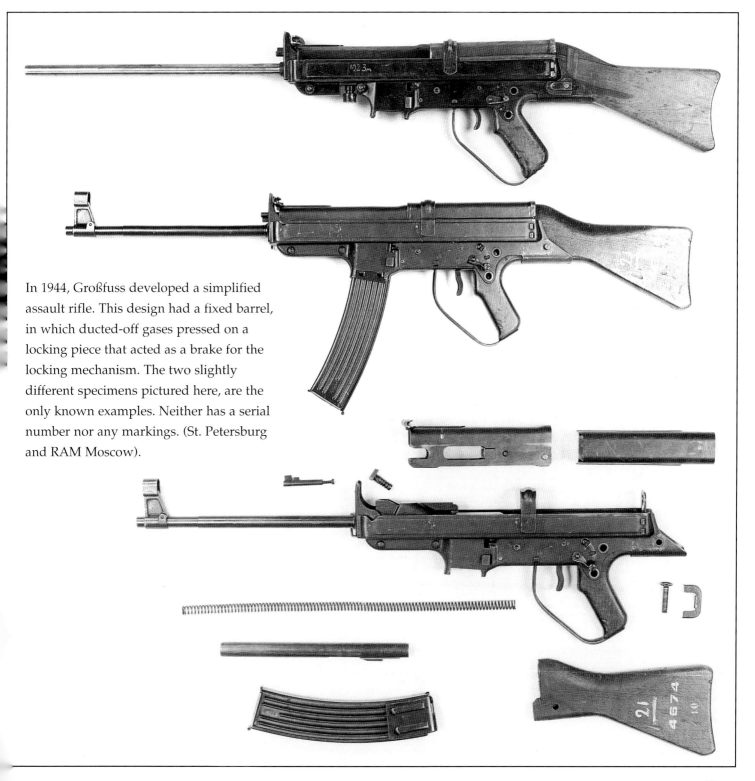

In 1944, Großfuss developed a simplified assault rifle. This design had a fixed barrel, in which ducted-off gases pressed on a locking piece that acted as a brake for the locking mechanism. The two slightly different specimens pictured here, are the only known examples. Neither has a serial number nor any markings. (St. Petersburg and RAM Moscow).

On August 27 and 28, 1944, the working group met at Großfuss in Döbeln, to discuss the projects of which prototypes or models were available. Among these were the retarded blow-back MP and the roller-locked MP from Mauser, the Großfuss MP, an MP from Steyr-Daimler-Puch and the Gustloff Models 507 and 508.

Großfuss

The Großfuss MP was a remarkable design with a fixed barrel, in which ducted-off gases pressed on a locking piece that acted as a brake for the breech mechanism. The weapon was designed by engineer V.G. Horn from Großfuss. The receiver, including the grip and magazine housing, consisted of only two parts, bended and welded together. Its configuration was described as a "disposable gun", with a weight of 3.9 kg. The description perfectly matches the two different guns pictured here. Neither of these show any marking, so it is difficult to say exactly when they were made. The proceedings of the working group state that by August, 1944, one prototype had been tested with 3000 rounds of ammunition and only the trigger group had given some problems. However, a document drawn up by Otto von Lossnitzer in 1947 states that the Großfuss MP was still in an experimental stage by the end of the war, but that it was further developed under Russian occupation.(17)

Steyr

The Steyr MP is described to have had a "turntable unlocked breech", with a magazine in the stock through which the cartridges were fed over a 90 degree angle in the barrel. The weight is given as 4.1 kg. The working group could not give an opinion about the qualities of the weapon, as only a hand-made prototype was ready, which lacked several parts, such as an extractor.

Gustloff

Then there were the two Gustloff Models 507 and 508. Both were gas-retarded blowback weapons. Model 507, described as a "pure disposable weapon", lacked a pistol grip, while Model 508 had a pistol grip similar to the MP 44. The frame consisted of two halves, welded together. The tubular breech was positioned around the barrel and recoiled in the way of a semi-automatic pistol. At the time, one prototype had been tested with 1,000 rounds without problems; four more prototypes would be ready in a few days. The Model 508 is described as similar to the 507, but having the pistol grip and sights of the MP 44. Both weapons may have resulted from trials held earlier by Gustloff to convert the MP 43 into a blow-back weapon.

Mauser

Finally there were the two Mauser models, variations of what is nowadays known as the *Gerät 06*. One was described as a recoil-operated weapon with a fixed barrel and a retarded roller-lock mechanism, with a weight of 3.9 kg, rounded sheet metal parts, a simplified trigger mechanism, ejection under an angle of 45 degrees downwards and 15 mm lower sights. One specimen had been made and tested with 1000 cartridges both in single shot and automatic fire without any notable failures.

The other Mauser design was a gas operated weapon with rigid roller locks, with a weight of 4 kg. Four prototypes had been made by August, 1944, which had been tested with some 30,000 rounds without notable failures.

Mauser had been working on these new machine pistols from at least October 1943 onward, although the roller-lock mechanism had been tested earlier on a Walther G43 in 7.92 x 57 mm.. The company's monthly

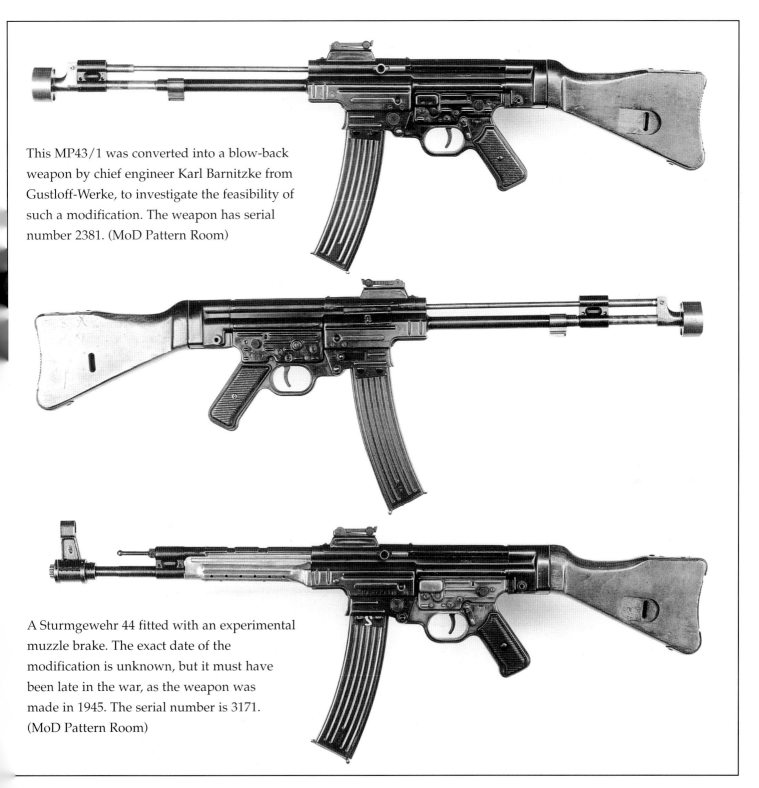

This MP43/1 was converted into a blow-back weapon by chief engineer Karl Barnitzke from Gustloff-Werke, to investigate the feasibility of such a modification. The weapon has serial number 2381. (MoD Pattern Room)

A Sturmgewehr 44 fitted with an experimental muzzle brake. The exact date of the modification is unknown, but it must have been late in the war, as the weapon was made in 1945. The serial number is 3171. (MoD Pattern Room)

reports, starting in November of that year, state that the construction of a weapon for the Patrone 43 was for 70 % ready, and that it had started the development of a completely new gun, for a 10.75 mm cartridge developed by DWM. Both developments were listed as company initiatives.

In November, 1943, Wa Prüf 2 I asked the Mauser company to investigate the possibility of a *Maschinenkarabiner* firing from an unlocked breech, which the company fitted in with its own developments. The December 1943 report lists several new projects: the self-loading rifles 02, 03 and 07 with roller-lock (the first being a study model, the second a G43 with roller-lock and the third a simplified construction), an MP with roller lock and the 10.75 mm MP, which was destined to have a retarded roller-lock. The latter was still under theoretical investigation.

In the course of January, 1944, it showed that a blow-back MP for the Patrone 43 was not feasible, but a first prototype of the roller-lock MP was made in February and was tried with 6000 cartridges the next month. Two more specimens were finished in April, which were handed over to Wa Prüf 2 for trials. As a result, some modifications were made. It should be noted here, however, that none of Mausers monthly reports mentions an order for a test-series of 30 weapons, as stated by several authors although 30 sets of components were made by April, 1945.

Although only prototypes of the Mauser weapons were ready by the Summer of 1944, the company aggressively pursued the adoption of its designs. At one of the meetings of the weapons committee, Mauser-director Weißenborn claimed it was "a crime" to continue production of the MP 44, as his company's weapon, named MP 45, was superior in both production and performance. In a letter to the *Reichsministerium*, dated June 27, 1944, the *Waffenamt* strongly opposed this point of view.(18) Although the Mauser design did represent a certain advance in the field of infantry firearms development, front troops were quite satisfied with the MP 44. Furthermore, the Waffenamt found that the Mauser design had several defects, which should be corrected first.

From a production point of view, the *Waffenamt* thought the receiver too complicated and the tolerances for the breechblock too small. Adoption of the MP45 would also require a complete re-tooling as only the magazine was interchangeable with the MP44. This was not advisable, as the MP45 would ultimately give an production advantage of no more than 20 percent over the MP44. Even if trials with the MP45 were successful, the *Waffenamt* favoured a greater production of the MP44 itself: *"Die Truppe ist an einer Umsteuerung auf das neue Modell der Firma Mauser überhaupt nicht interessiert"* (the troops are not in the least interested in changing over to the new model of the Mauser company).

The working group judged that none of the designs presented showed sufficient advantages over the MP 44, to justify adoption. It was suggested to simplify the MP 44 itself as far as possible. Meanwhile, the designs of Großfuss, the Gustloff 507 and the semi-rigid Mauser designs were recommended for further development and a possible suitability for other calibers, due to the novelty of their designs.

Two developments

The *Sonderkommission Infanteriewaffen* could not completely agree to these conclusions. In its meeting on August 29 and 30, 1944, held at Großfuss in Döbeln, the weapons previously studied in the working group were

In 1944, the Mauser company developed two types of simplified assault rifles. The weapon pictured here, serial number 3, features rigid roller locks. (MoD Pattern Room)

In the final stages of World War II, many German companies produced highly simplified weapons. The field-stripped gun pictured here was made by Gustloff, and has most characteristics of their Model 507. This weapon is often quite mistakenly called VG 1-5. Official *Volksgewehr* (VG) designations were as follows: VG1 – Walther, VG2- Spreewerke, VG3 – Rheinmetall, VG4 – Mauser-Werke, and VG5 – Steyr. (MoD Pattern Room)

demonstrated to the full committee. Engineer Altenburger presented the two Mauser designs, engineer Horn the Großfuss model, and Dr. Maier held a speech on the possibilities of an unlocked breech in combination with the Patrone 43. Furthermore, the meeting discussed ongoing simplifications of the MP 44 by Erma and Haenel. The committee decided to continue both developments simultaneously: a study towards possible production simplifications of the MP 44, and the development of a simpler MP by Großfuss and Mauser. These should give a production advantage of at least 50 percent.

This decision was quite disappointing for the Mauser company, whose monthly report states that it "complicated the competition with the MP44". Even as late as August, 1944, competition among German companies was stiff. At the same time, Haenel's director Schmeisser staged a successful coup. He got the committee to agree that "alien companies would not get involved in the further development of devices, without consulting the mother company", thus effectively blocking the initiatives of ERMA.(19)

At the committee meeting, Schmeisser elaborated on the ongoing simplification and development projects. In the course of 1943, several experimental versions had already been developed, with different models of flash supressors and different rear sight positions. These had all been discarded. The present projects included a hold-open device by means of the magazine follower; a simplified receiver; a new gas cylinder cap for the use of a rifle grenade launcher; a simplified breech block and extractor; a simplified breech block guide; a new attachment of the front sight; a new attachment of the stock; a wire-cutter; modification of the weapon for use in tanks without stock, but with a folding frontsight and

a different position of the main spring; a main spring placed outside the stock; a shortened, one-piece bolt carrier, and a closed groove for the cocking handle combined with a fixed position of the cocking handle during fire. Apart from these, Haenel documents list the following experiments for 1944 and 1945: sights and parts of the trigger mechanism made from powder metals, hammered barrels from Appel in Spandau and sinter-iron barrels from Neumeyer in Nuremberg, a 60 shot magazine, a gas tube from rolled sheet metal and a mount for an infrared aiming device, named the *UR-Gerät*, which had been developed by the *Forschungsanstalt der Reichspost*.

At least one gun (numbered V9) incorporating some of these changes is known to exist, although it has been erroneously dated at late 1943.(20) Some of the simplifications, however, did reach the production stage. Some 1945-production guns lack one of the reinforcing ribs on the frame, just above the magazine housing. This development seems to have been further pursued in a gun marked "MP45" and numbered 89/A in which the part of the receiver above the magazine housing has been completely redesigned.

The last documented evidence about the *Maschinenkarabiner* development comes from the Mauser report of December, 1944. It states that in January, 1945, all companies should present models, naming Großfuss, Rheinmetall and Haenel as the competitors. No exact information is available as to the nature of these weapons, but it may be safely assumed that in the last months of the war a rather extensive amount of development work was undertaken.

From 1944 onward, the Haenel company was working on possible simplifications in the Sturmgewehr design. This weapon, marked MP45, shows some of these simplifications, such as a redesigned receiver. The serial number is 89/A. (Courtesy dr G. Sturgess)

VI TECHNICAL DESCRIPTION

The *Sturmgewehr* mechanism

The main parts of the MP43, MP44 and the *Sturmgewehr* are the receiver, the barrel, gas chamber, gas piston, breechblock, recoil spring, handguard, stock and the grip assembly which contains the firing mechanism. The mechanism has three control elements: the trigger, the fire-selector and the safety catch. The conventional safety has two positions: up is safe and down is the fire position. The fire-selector is a push-through button. If it is pushed to the right the gun fires automatic, if it is pushed to the left the weapon fires single shots. The button is marked with E and D (*Einzelfeuer* and *Dauerfeuer*).

When a loaded magazine is in place and the gun has been cocked, the working is as follows:

When the trigger is pressed, the hammer is released to strike the inertia firing pin. This is a wedge-shaped pin that does not have a conventional spring, as it is primer-retracted.

As the bullet passes the gas-port in the barrel, the gas expands into the gas chamber and drives a piston to the rear. For a short distance, the piston can move without interfering with the locking of the weapon. A gas vent in the top of the gas chamber permits the gas to escape once the gas end of the pistol clears it.

After a short rearward travel the bolt carrier hook picks up the separate bolt member, mounted below it, and pulls it up and back to perform the unlocking action. The rearward movement of the bolt compresses the recoil spring, extending back into the stock. The moving bolt ejects the empty cartridge case and cocks the hammer.

Field stripping

The magazine must be removed and it must be made sure the weapon is not loaded. A spring-held pin passes through the receiver and stock, connecting the two. When this pin is pulled out from the right side, the stock may be withdrawn, exposing the recoil spring. The grip unit swings down on its hinge. If the cocking handle is now retracted, the recoil spring, bolt, bolt carrier and pistol will be brought back for removal.

For cleaning, the gas cup which closes the front of the gas tube must be unscrewed, using the dismantling tool. The bolt can be lifted of the bolt carrier and the extractor and firing pin removed.

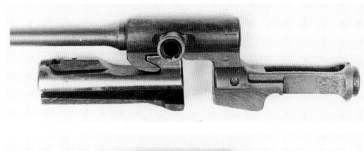

The heart of the Sturmgewehr: the bolt guiding piece and the bolt in locked and unlocked position. (Brussels)

A drawing of the Sturmgewehr mechanism.

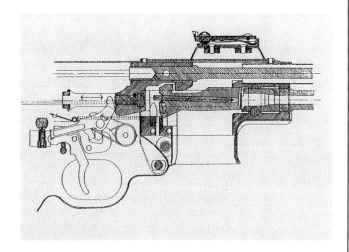

This close-up shows the controls of the Sturmgewehr: the magazine release button, the trigger, the safety catch (set on *Feuer*) and the fire control button. (Brussels).

VII ACCESSORIES AND AMMUNITION

The basis accessories for the MP43, MP44 and *Sturmgewehr* consisted of six magazines, a magazine loading tool, a sling, three muzzle covers, a dismantling tool to unscrew the gas cilinder plug and remove the handguard, a cleaning brush for the gas cilinder and several spare parts, such as an extractor, extractor spring, extractor pin, a firing pin and a manual.

Telescopic sights

In the early stages of *Maschinenkarabiner* development, the Army authorities had not yet quite decided which role it had to play. Some advocated the role of a general purpose gun, which should replace the pistol, the selfloading rifle, the MP38 and 40 submachine guns, the K98 rifle, the K98 with rifle grenade launcher, the K98 with telescopic sight, and possibly even the light machine gun. In November, 1942, the Army High Command proposed a full-scale troop trial to get a clearer view of the weapon's possibilities. One squad of each of five divisions had to be equipped with nine MKb 42s and one MG42. From these MKb's, one had to have a telescopic sight and one a rifle grenade launcher.

Although this troop trial was never held, it may well be the explanation for the fact that all MKb 42 (H) got rails on the side of the rear sight, on which a special mount with a ZF 41 could be placed. The only known specimen of such a mount is marked with the logo of the Merz Werke.

Putting scope rails on a weapon is one thing, but making a precision rifle is quite another. The MKb 42 fired from an open bolt and therefore lacked the accuracy needed in a sniper weapon. It was not until October, 1943, that the Infantry School tested the precision of the improved MP43/1 in comparison with a G43. Both were equipped with the ZF4 scope which had been developed earlier that year.

For the occasion, the MP43/1 with serial number 918 had gotten a mounting rail on the left side of the receiver, similar to that on the G43. The repositioning of the rail was necessary because of the smaller eye relief of the ZF4, as compared to the ZF 41. The combination of weapon and mount proved useless. After firing thirty rounds fully automatic, the optics were completely dislocated. Of five single shots fired afterwards, none came even near the target.(21) As a result of this test, WaPrüf 2 ordered another twenty hand-made mounts with improved clamps, which were to be ready by November. However, it was not until February, 1944, that the Infantry School could continue its trials, this time with ten MP43/1's and six G43s. The serial numbers of the MPs were noted as follows: 7491 b, 7492 b, 7494 b, 7495 b, 7497 b, 7500 b, 7503 b, 7504 b, 7506 b and 7507 b, but only the best three of these were actually used.

The test showed that the quality of the ZF 4 scopes left much to be desired. Apart from that, the MP43/1 did not perform as should be expected from a sniper rifle. Extended trials could have given a solution, but these were never held. The last mention of a scoped MP was in September, 1944, when an MP44 with Voigtländer ZF 4 was shown to the authorities as part of a larger demonstration of infantry weapons. By then, however, *Reichsminister* Albert Speer for Armament and Military Production had formed a commission for infantry weapons, which focussed on the improvement of the K43 as a sniper rifle. No further telescope developments for the MP44 are mentioned in its proceedings.

A *Sturmgewehr* 44 with a rifle grenade launcher.
From the MP43 onward, the weapons could be
equipped with the standard *Gewehrgranatgerät*, but
the grenade sight required a special mounting.
A suitable solution was never found.
(Courtesy H.B. Lockhoven)

An MP43 equipped with a ZF 41 scope and
a special mount. Various experiments were
made with scopes and mounts, but the
MP's were not suited for a sniper role.
(Courtesy W. Odegaard)

An MP44 with a ZF4 telescopic sight. Some
trials were held with these sights in the
course of 1943 and 1944, but it soon showed
that the K98k and the K43 were far superior
as sniper weapons. This weapon has serial
number 2680. (MoD Pattern Room)

Grenade launcher

While the efforts to turn the *Maschinenkarabiner* into a sniper rifle had failed completely, the development of a suitable rifle grenade launcher was only slightly more succesful. The earliest models had a threaded muzzle end, protected by a knurled nut, as on the MP38 and 40. It seems this was done to fit a blank firing device, similar to that of the submachine guns. Some pictures exist of a screw-on rifle grenade launcher, mounted on a MKb 42 (W), but it soon became clear that this was not a feasible construction.

By August, 1943, the front part of the barrel of the MP43 was stepped-down to except the standard K98k *Gewehrgranatgerät*. This change in production, however, did not mean that the MP43 was used with a rifle grenade launcher from that time onward. The weapon fired a different type of cartridge than the K98, so a suitable grenade cartridge had to be developed. Furthermore, the MP was a semi-automatic weapon which needed a special device to give sufficient pressure to the rifle grenade.

By July, 1944, the problems with the cartridges seemed to have been solved. Two types had been developed, one with a 1.5 gram charge for the *Gewehrsprenggranate* and one with a 1.9 gram charge for the *Gewehrpanzergranate*. A suitable plug to block the semi-automatic mechanism gave more problems. In September, 1944, the Haenel company was still working on this and it was only in January, 1945, that the authorities could report that the technical aspects has been solved. A plug, replacing the screw cap closing the gas cilinder, blocked the gas vent, thus making the MP a single-shot weapon. In March and April, 1945, a test was held with the StG 44 and the *Gewehrgranatgerät*. Both functioned satisfactorily. One month later, however, the war was over.

The curved barrels

Without doubt the most remarkable accessory of the *Sturmgewehr* was the curved barrel device. This existed in two versions. The so-called *Vorsatz J* (the J to read as I, for Infantry) had a 30-degree curving and was destined to be fired from trenches and the like. The *Vorsatz Pz (Panzer)* had a 90-degree curving and was destined to be used in tanks and armoured vehicles.

The curved barrel was a very ingenious solution to an old problem: how to fire at an enemy from complete cover? The advent of tanks and armoured cars had given this problem a new dimension. These vehicles were armed, of course, but when an enemy came close enough, this armament was useless. Without infantry support, a tank could simply be destroyed by the application of magnetic mines or the like, its crew literally being trapped.

The solution for this problem was found by Colonel Hans-Joachim Schaede, head of the production department of Speer's ministry. Late in 1943, Schaede suggested to attach a curved barrel to an MG34, so that tanks could defend themselves more effectively.

By the end of 1943, Rheinmetall had been given the order to develop a curved barrel attachment and test it with all 7.92 x 57 mm weapons. The German infantry cartridge, however, soon proved far too powerful for whatever curved barrel. Although some attachments were made for the MG34, these all broke down after less than a hundred shots. Then someone got a bright idea: wouldn't the curved barrel function better with the 7.92 x 33 mm cartridge? This had a shorter bullet and a lower pressure. Some trials showed that the short cartridge suited itself far better to the idea and as the *Sturmgewehr* was the only weapon at the time which fired that cartridge, attention focused on this particular weapon.

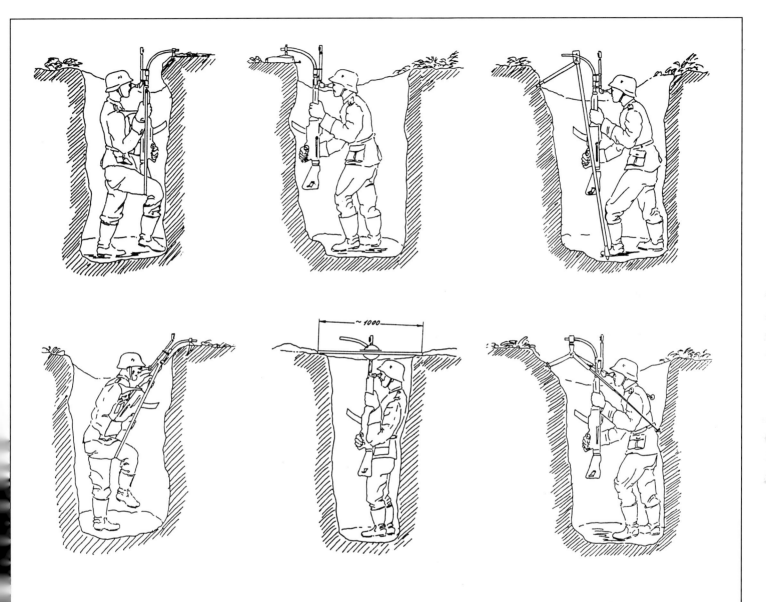

In August, 1944, the company of Rheinmetall-Borsig made six rather inventive designs for a *Sturmgewehr* with a curved barrel device. The six sketches are pictured here. (Militärarchiv Freiburg)

In July, 1944, a *Sturmgewehr* and a curved barrel attachment were demonstrated to the highest officers. This first attachment consisted of a rifled barrel with some gas vent holes, bent over an angle of 90 degrees. Its precision was quite satisfactory. Fired single shot at a distance of 100 metres, all projectiles landed in a 30 centimeter square. The barrel attachment was estimated to have a 2000 rounds service life.

The demonstration must have made a considerable impression. On August 8, the chief of the *Heereswaffenamt* ordered the production on 10,000 pieces as soon as possible. This was somewhat premature. In the meantime it had become clear that a 90 degree angle suited the needs of tanks and armoured vehicles, but less those of the infantry. At a meeting at Rheinmetall, on August 25, it was therefore decided to design a second version, curved between 30 to 45 degrees, with a weight of no more than two kilograms and a service life of approximately 5000 rounds. The device should have an attachment similar to that of the rifle grenade launcher and a simple mirror sight, with which the weapon could be fired from the hip. A test with ten of these devices would show which model was most suitable.

On October 27, 1944, representatives of the *Waffenamt*, Speer's ministry, and the companies of Rheinmetall, Bush, Zeiss and Bergmann, met at the Rheinmetall testing grounds in Unterlüss to investigate the different models of curved barrel attachments.(23) There were demonstrations with curving of 30 and 90 degrees and several optical aiming devices. Furthermore the party investigated whether it was possible to fire rifle grenades. For this, the Germans had found an ingenious solution. The vent holes in the curved barrel could be closed with a special sleeve, so that the cartridge gave enough pressure. The results, however, were disappointing. The standard rifle grenade retained its range of about 250 meters, but its accuracy fell dramatically. A target of 1.5 by 1 meter, put at 75 meters, was impossible to hit.

The meeting in October gave no direct result. A curving of 30 degrees with a mirror aiming device attached to the weapon, seemed the most suitable for infantry use, but at least a small troop trial was needed for a final decision. It was therefore decided to send six barrels and two sets of three different types of aiming devices to the Infantry School at Döberitz for a further evaluation. With some delay, the devices were sent to Döberitz in mid-November 1944. The Infantry School got four versions: two barrels with the iron sights mounted on the left and the mirrors on the barrel, two barrels with the iron sights on top and the mirrors on the handguard of the weapon, a barrel with the iron sights on the left and one with the sights on top, both in combination with an aiming device on the helmet. The trial was to last only a few days and had to show which combination suited best. Furthermore, the Infantry School had to investigate durability, precision and the possibilities for cover.

By the end of November, 1944, the Infantry School reported that none of the models had performed well. The aiming devices were not solid enough and were constructed in such a manner that the weapon had to be fired from the hip. This prevented adequate cover. Nonetheless, the School found the principle quite practical.

On December 8, 1944, representatives of the *Waffenamt*, Rheinmetall-Borsig and Zeiss met again, to discuss an improved version of the curved barrel device, by then baptised *Vorsatz J*.(24) It was decided to further evaluate three models: a 30 degree curved barrel with a prismatic sight developed by Zeiss, and a 45 degree curved barrel with both this prismatic sight and a set of mirrors. The

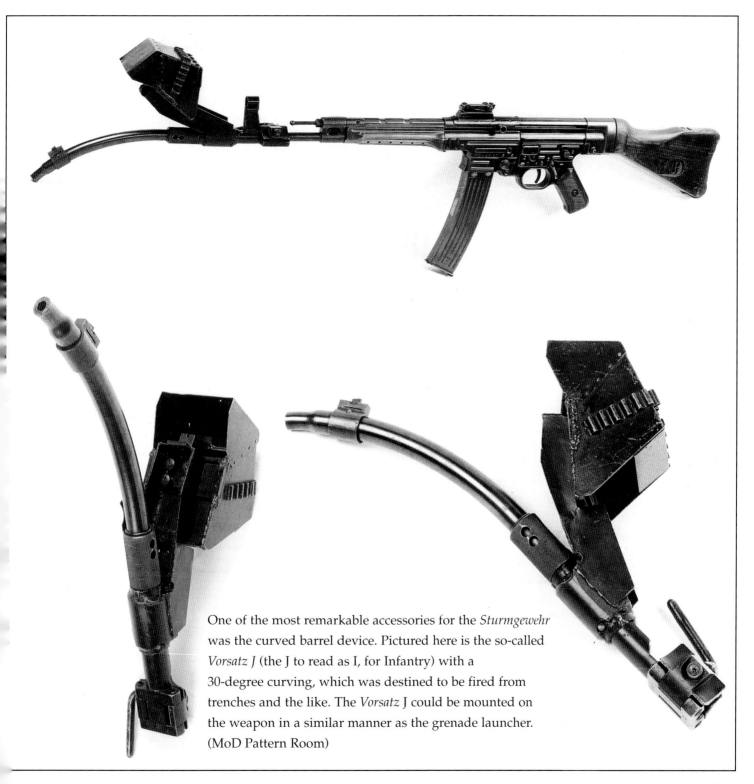

One of the most remarkable accessories for the *Sturmgewehr* was the curved barrel device. Pictured here is the so-called *Vorsatz J* (the J to read as I, for Infantry) with a 30-degree curving, which was destined to be fired from trenches and the like. The *Vorsatz J* could be mounted on the weapon in a similar manner as the grenade launcher. (MoD Pattern Room)

latter two were, however, only intended to test the aiming device, as trials at Rheinmetall had shown that the stronger curving gave excessive recoil. A sufficient quantity of the three devices had to be delivered to the Infantry School before December 21, 1944. Before Christmas it could thus be decided of which model a 0-series of 3000 pieces would be made. Pending this decision, Rheinmetall was ordered to manufacture 1000 curved barrels in January.

This planning was rather optimistic. The improved version of the curved barrel attachment still functioned rather poorly. The 30-degree barrel broke after only 300 rounds and the 45-degree barrels performed even worse. The attachment of the front sight broke after 7 and 10 rounds respectively and part of the muzzle was torn off after 170 rounds. The attachment of the barrel to the weapon bent and the whole configuration had an excessive recoil. On December 24, 1944, it was decided to continue the test with only the 30-degree barrel. Rheinmetall was to make 200 pieces, half of which with the possibility to attach the grenade cup.

Ultimately, the company produced only 100 pieces, the exact configuration of which is unknown. The Infantry School, the *Panzertruppenschule*, the *Gebirgsjägerschule* and the *SS-Panzertruppenschule* were informed that they could each collect 25 pieces from Rheinmetall from March 31 onward. Their trials reports were to be handed in by May, 1945, but by then the war was over.

There are widely varying estimates of the number of curved barrel devices produced. Some authors claim that 10,000 pieces were made, but this was only an initial production estimate. From the information given before, it may be concluded that no more than 100 to 150 pieces of the *Vorsatz J* were ever made. Little can be said for certain about the *Vorsatz Pz*, the 90 degree barrel for tanks. By October, 1944, the parties concerned had not yet agreed about the usefulness of this device. According to one source, about 550 pieces were ready in early 1945.

The Deckungszielgerät

More or less simultaneously to the curved barrels, another device was tested to fire the *Sturmgewehr* from complete cover. This device was called the *Deckungszielgerät 45*. It consisted of a holder in which the weapon was fastened with two metal clips, an extra metal stock with a wooden grip, a transfer device for the trigger and two mirrors, placed at a 45 degree angle towards the bore axis. To transport the device, the mirrors could be detached and the lower mirror holder and the stock could be folded. The upper mirror holder had a fixed position, in order to facilitate adjustment.

The existence of such a device has been documented for the K98k, the Gewehr 41 and 43, and even the MG34, but it was little known that it was made for the *Sturmgewehr* as well. This is not surprising, because it is unlikely that more than twenty pieces were ever made.

The *Deckungszielgerät* for the *Sturmgewehr* seems to have been developed by the Gustloff company in late 1944, as a specimen was demonstrated in September of that same year.(25) A troop trial was deemed necessary, but this did not take place until some six months later. At the end of March, 1945, the Infantry School at Grafenwöhr, the *Panzertruppenschule*, the *Gebirgsjägerschule* and the *SS-Panzertruppenschule* each were informed that they had to collect four pieces of the *Deckungszielgerät* in Döberitz for a test together with the *Vorsatz J*. This test should prove which of the two devices performed best. As far as known, the pictures published here are the only remaining evidence of the *Deckungszielgerät*.

These pictures, from March, 1945, show the *Deckungs-zielgerät* 45, a device with which the *Sturmgewehr* could be fired from complete cover. Developed in the final stages of the war, it is unlikely that more than twenty pieces were made.
(Militärarchiv Freiburg)

Magazines and magazine pouches

The ammunition supply that each man was to carry with his *Maschinenkarabiner* was established at 180 cartridges, carried in six magazines. The magazines were stacked in two pouches. The first model of these pouches was made of fabric and the body had three compartments, which were closed by one single large flap, secured by a strap and buckle.

During troop trials, the model of these pouches was heavily criticized. Because of the single flap, both outer magazines could easily be lost, and the pouches were not sufficiently protected from rain. A new model was developed, with three separate flaps. This was approved in late 1943, but production seems only to have commenced a year later. The picture section of this books shows a large quantity of old model pouches, or soldiers carrying an MP but no pouches at all. Of the new model, several varieties are known, some made completely out of fabric, others with leather reinforced parts.

The magazine loading tool

The magazine loading tool was a simple spoon-like piece of sheet metal. One end could be placed over the top of the magazine, the other end was formed in such a way that a five round clip could be inserted. By simply pressing downwards on the cartridges, these were fed into the magazine. The loading tool was discarded in March, 1945, as the cartridges were to be packed without clips from then onward.

Ammunition

The 7,9 x 33 mm catridge (or *Pistolenpatrone* 43 as it was commonly called) was designed by Polte-Magdeburg. It received its final form in 1941, with a 33 mm case and a bullet of 25.8 mm.

It seems that during 1941 and 1942, Polte was the only manufacturer, but as the need for ammunition rose, other companies were introduced. The cartridge was exclusively made with a lacquered steel case, the only variations being the use of a reinforced base (marked St +) and a single flash-hole (marked – St). Although tool cartridges and dummies seem to have been made in some quantity, all other types (such as tracer and rifle grenade cartridges) were made experimentally only.

The headstamp of the cartridge case offers information on the origin of the case: the manufacturer' code, the date and lot of production and the case material. The manufacturer's code consisted of a two- or three-letter code. The following manufacturers are known:

Code	Manufacturer
ak	Munitionswerken vorm. Sellier & Bellot Prag, Werk Vlasim, Protektorat
aux	Polte, Werk Magdeburg
dou.	Waffenwerke Brünn AG, Werk Povazska Bystrica, Protektorat
eej	Märkisches Walzwerk GmbH, Werk Strausberg, Potsdam
fva	Draht- und Metallwarenfabrik GmbH, Salzwedel
hla	Metallwarenfabrik Treuenbritzen GmbH, Werk Sebaldushof
kam	Hasag Hugo Schneider Eisen- und Metallwerke GmbH, Werk Skarsysko-Kamienna, Gen. Gouvernement
oxo	Teuto Metallwerke GmbH, Osnabrück
wa	Hasag Hugo Schneider AG, Werk Leipzig
de	Hasag Hugo Schneider AG, Werk Leipzig in 1945.

Intermediate cartridges. From left to right: 7.5 x 35 mm Swiss (1920's), 7.9 x 45 mm (Polte), 7 x 45 mm (Polte), 7.75 x 39,5 (Genschow), 7.92 x 30 (Polte), and some variations of the Kurzpatrone: ball, tracer, rifle grenade, dummy and a cutaway. (D.W. Zoetmulder)

One of the variations of the magazine pouch. (Politiemuseum Apeldoorn)

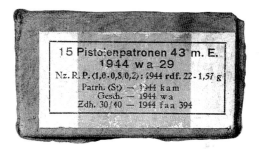

A typical box for 15 Sturmgewehr cartridges, designated Pistolenpatronen 43. (D.W. Zoetmulder)

The cover of a Sturmgewehr manual. (H.L. Visser)

VIII PRODUCTION, CODES AND MARKINGS

As for any war-time German weapon, many pages can be filled with *Sturmgewehr* figures. Many departments kept their own administration of production, acceptance, stock, losses and the like. These figures seem very accurate, but as the war progressed, facts and fiction became more and more intertwined, so they must be considered with caution.

As far as the MKb 42 from Walther is concerned: despite the fact that some authors claim that as many as 8,000 pieces were made, all available evidence suggests that no more (and probably less) than the initial 200 prototypes were produced, the larger part of these still remaining at the Walther factory at the end of the war.

The MKb 42 (H) was made in larger quantities. By March, 1943, 2734 weapons had been accepted. At that time, production estimates were as follows: 2000 in April, 3000 in May, 3000 in June and a final 1000 in July. These estimates correspond reasonably accurate with the actual acceptance figures of 2179 in April and 3044 in May. As the figures for June onward include both the MKb 42 (H) and the first quantities of the MP 43/1, the exact number of MKb's is unknown. However, if the estimates are taken as true figures, the total would be some 12,000 Haenel MKb's.

Production of the MP43/1 commenced in June, 1943, and was apparently stopped in December, in favour of the MP43. Production and acceptance figures make no clear division between the two models, but an educated guess of about 14,000 MP43/1's can be made.

There is no possible distinction in production between the MP43, the MP44 and the *Sturmgewehr*. Production figures have been recorded up until April, 1945. By then, some 415,000 weapons had been assembled. The production figure for April is unknown, but as the Third Reich had nearly crumbled by then, the grand total may be estimated at something between 420,000 and 440,000 guns. This conforms with a statement made by Hugo Schmeisser just after the war. According to the Haenel director, a total of 424,000 MPs was produced, divided over the following assembling companies:

Haenel	code fxo	185,000
Sauer & Sohn	code ce	55,000
Erma	code qlv	104,000
Steyr	code bnz	80,000

The most notable thing about this list is that there is no mention of Mauser. According to Schmeisser, assembly was only getting started at the Mauser factory in Borsigwalde, near Berlin, at the end of the war, but a quantity of MP's seems to have been made in Oberndorf as well.

The production figures for all types of *Maschinenkarabiner*, as given in the monthly *"Uberblick über den Rüstungsstand von Waffen"* (Survey of required and accepted amount of small arms) are as follows:

November 1942	25	September 1943	190
December 1942	91	October 1943	4000
January 1943	500	November 1943	6200
February 1943	1217	December 1943	6493
March 1943	900	January 1944	340
April 1943	2179	February 1944	4050
May 1943	3044	March 1944	7000
June 1943	1898	April 1944	9000
July 1943	1423	May 1944	9500
August 1943	366	June 1944	13,000

The awt-code of the Württembergische Metallwarenfabrik AG
on the left side of the receiver of
an MP43. (Brussels)

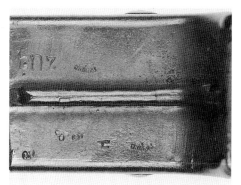

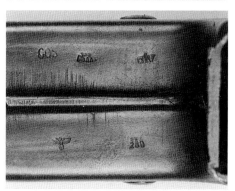

The markings of four MP assembly companies: fxo for Haenel (MP 43,
7015g/44), bnz for Steyr-Daimler-Puch (MP44, 8885/44), ce for Sauer en Sohn
(MP44, 5606p/ 44) and qlv for the Erma company (MP44, 9206ab/45). Note that
the Steyr receiver lacks the cos-mark of the Merz-Werke in Frankfurt. (Brussels)

Two examples of serial numbers on MPs. Left is the marking on the receiver, and at the right the number as it appears
on the butt. The magazine release button on the left is chequered, while later examples had concentric rings. (Brussels)

July 1944	20,150	December 1944	49,800	
August 1944	29,500	January 1945	41,683	
September 1944	35,000	February 1945	34,300	
October 1944	48,000	March 1945	48,633	
November 1944	55,100			

Subcontractors

Production of the Sturmgewehr was subcontracted on a hitherto unknown scale. Literally dozens of firms made components, some engaging in only one simple part, other in various and more complex ones. A complete listing is impossible, but a document drawn up by Haenel shortly after the war gives extended information. Haenel itself made the following parts: extractor, ejector, grip, stock, barrel, firing pin, gas chamber, magazine housing, and breechblock. According to a *"Verzeichnis unser Unterlieferanten für Stg 44 mit Angaben der von diesen Firmen gefertigten Teilen"* (listing of our subcontractors for the Stg 44), drawn up shortly after the war, other parts were made by the following companies: (26)

- National Krupp-Registrierkassen GmbH, Berlin-Neuköln (cnd)
- Waasia-Ofenwerk Recke & Co, Haynau (cxt)
- Venus-Waffenwerk, Zella-Mehlis
- Moritz & Gerstenberger, Zella-Mehlis (ghk)
- Fr. Langenhahn, Zella-Mehlis
- Gebr. Kempt Gewehrfabrik, Suhl
- J.P. Sauer & Sohn, Suhl (ce)
- Erma-Werke, Erfurt (ayf, later qlv)
- Luck & Wagner, Suhl (k)
- Curt Wartz & Co, Zella Mehlis (cq)
- C.W. Meinel-Scholer, Klingenthal (euh)
- Merz-Werke, Frankfurt (cos)
- Mauser-Werke, Oberndorf (byf)

- Steyr-Daimler-Puch, Werk Steyr (bnz.)
- Deutsche Kühl- und Kraftmaschinen GmbH, Scharfenstein (ehs)
- Boehme & Co, Minden (dwc)
- Otto Jaeger, Siegmar-Schönau
- Progreß-Werk, Oberkirch (bpp.)
- Württembergische Metallwarenfabrik, Geislingen (awt)
- R. Peter, Schmalkalden
- AEG, Hennisdorf (enl)
- Dübelwerke KG, Berlin
- Vereinigte Isolatorenwerke AG, Berlin (gbm)
- Tischlerei Wickes, Suhl
- R. und O. Lux, Bad Liebenstein (aqr)
- Waffenfabrik C. Eickhorn, Solingen (cof)
- Erste Nordböhmische Metallwarenfabrik, Niedereinsiedel (jvd)
- "Pallas-Werke", Barchfeld (jjn)
- C.R. Ebert, Suhl
- Gewehrfabrik Greifelt, Suhl (lhr)
- C. Herm. Nendel, Chemnitz
- G. Anschütz, Zella Mehlis
- Gustloff-Werke, Suhl (dfb)
- Gebr. Merkel, Suhl
- Astra-Werke AG, Chemnitz (l)
- Carl Rohrseitz, Zirndorf
- H.B. Schlothauer, Ruhla (dpu)
- Diana Mayer & Grammelspacher, Rastatt (lxr)
- Christoph Funk, Suhl
- Schmidt & Habermann, Suhl
- A. Kron, Solingen
- Spree-Werke, Grottau (cyq)
- Emil Zehner Metallwarenfabrik, Suhl
- Paul Henkel, Mäbendorf
- R. Kreisel, Gablonz (btt)

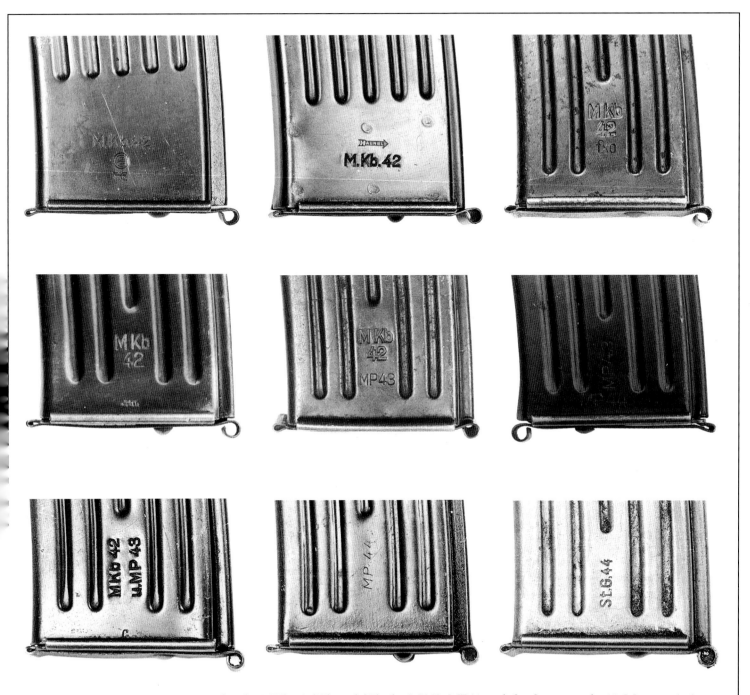

Different markings on magazines for the MKb 42 (W) and (H), the MP43, MP44 and the *Sturmgewehr* 44. More varieties and combinations exist, with one remarkable exception: although there are weapons with the MP43/1 designation, there are no known magazines marked accordingly.

IX PROPAGANDA PICTURES

The pictures on the following pages are a special selection, depicting the *Sturmgewehr* in use. Composing this section was not easy, as *Sturmgewehr* pictures are quite scarce. The main reason for this is simple: it was not until the Summer of 1944 that larger quantities of the weapon reached the front. Thus, the *Sturmgewehr* was only used in the last year of the war, when the situation for the Germans became more and more chaotic.

This situation clearly shows in the type of pictures. Although there are quite a few posed photos, the larger part can be categorized more as combat pictures rather than pure propaganda photos. Apart from a demonstration of several weapons to high officers, there is a complete lack of images of recreational shooting, training and the like. In the last year of the war, there were apparently very few quiet moments.

Some of the pictures show soldiers carrying an MKb 42 (H), as late as March, 1945. This is remarkable, as the MKb was a trials weapon only, which fired from an open bolt and therefore lacked the single-shot accuracy of the *Sturmgewehr*. Maybe the soldiers favoured even a trials weapon over a K98k or an MP 38 or 40.

In the following section, some pictures have been included to demonstrate the overal situation in which the *Sturmgewehr* was used. The Propaganda pictures feature Germans with Russian submachine guns and even an American Thompson, all of which were used to increase firepower – a role which the *Sturmgewehr* should have played, if sufficient quantities of weapon and ammunition had been available.

From April to June, 1942, the Infantry School at Döberitz tested 25 pieces of the Haenel *Maschinenkarabiner* 42.
Several pictures were taken during these trials, clearly showing some of the characteristics of these weapons. This trials
gun lacks an ejection port cover and a handguard. Also note the unusual configuration of the upper part of the spare
magazine, laying in the foreground.
Döberitz, 1942
(Militärarchiv Freiburg)

During the tests in the Summer of 1942, the Infantry School developed fabric pouches to carry the ammuntion supply of six magazines. Each pouch had three compartments, which were closed by a single large flap. As this proved not satisfactory, a new model with a separate flap for each compartment was developed, but this was produced in quantity only from late 1944 onward.
Döberitz, 1942
(Militärarchiv Freiburg)

In case the ammuntion supply with each Sturmgewehr would be more than 180 cartridges (six magazines), the Infantry School suggested an additional pouch, to be carried on the back, just above the belt. From the look of it, this pouch contained two more magazines. It was never adopted.
Döberitz, 1942
(Militärarchiv Freiburg)

These two pictures from the 1942-trials show the proposed fabric magazine pouch, containing three magazines. The large single flap proved impractical, as it gave insufficient protection and the magazines on the left and right fell out easily. Yet it would not be until late 1944 that an improved model, with a separate flap for each magazine compartment, was made in quantity.
Döberitz, 1942
(Militärarchiv Freiburg)

The rear of the proposed magazine pouch. The Infantry School soon found that the most comfortable way to carry the pouches was oblique, as this way the pouches did not hinder the soldier when firing from a prone position. Several varieties of the magazine pouches were eventually used, as shown later in this picture section.
Döberitz, 1942
(Militärarchiv Freiburg)

These two photos, shot by SS-photographer Fritsch, are a classical example of the way in which the Germans made their propaganda pictures. The original caption reads: "The fight of our grenadiers and SS-cavalry is marked by a relentless harshness. Every house becomes a fiercely battled point of resistance. These men, who do not yield an inch and inflict the heaviest and bloodiest losses upon the enemy, perform heroic actions, which will some time be known."
In sharp contrast to these lines, the soldier is not only cleanly shaven, but the ejection port cover of his Sturmgewehr is closed as well, meaning the gun is probably not cocked.
Budapest, January 1945.
(Museum of Modern History, Slovenia No. 5887/10)

In this second picture, photographer Fritsch entered the house for a different angle, with equally dramatic effect. The original caption is exactly the same as with the picture on the previous page.
Budapest, January 1945.
(Museum of Modern History, Slovenia No. 6618/16)

A group of well-clad Mountain Troops is adressed by General-Oberst Walther Model decorated with the Knight's Cross with oak leaves and swords. The man on the right carries an MKb 42 (H), of which the muzzle end with the characteristic elongated gas plug is just visible. Also note that this weapon has a bayonet lug.

Northern Russia, Spring 1944.

(Bundesarchiv Koblenz No. 701/376/5A)

A *Feldwebel* with a *Maschinenkarabiner* 42 looks amused in the distance. Among his decorations are a *Infanterieabzeichen* (Infantry badge), *Heeresdienstauszeichen* (Service badge), and a wound badge in black. As this picture was taken in the Summer of 1943, he must have been of the first soldiers to get an MKb 42 (H). Note that the weapon is cocked. As the MKb 42 fired from an open bolt, the cocking handle is in the rear position.

Northern Russia, Summer of 1943.

(Bundesarchiv Koblenz No. 698/49/27A)

These two pictures show a group of mountain troops with dogs. They may have been taken during an exercise with dog sleds. All men are equipped with MP's. Note that the magazine pouches still have one single flap, which provided insufficient protection. A new model with separate flaps for each compartment had been developed by late 1943, but mass-production commenced only a year later.

Russia, January/February 1944.

(Bundesarchiv Koblenz No. 692/253/11)

This *Gebirgsjäger* fastens the belts of the dog. As this picture clearly shows, he carries an MP43/1, recognizable by its straight barrel. The gun has a muzzle cover and looks quite new.
Russia, January/February 1944.
(Bundesarchiv Koblenz No. 692/253/24)

These two pictures were apparently taken to demonstrate some of the finer MP details. Although the original caption has been lost, it is easy to imagine something like "Our new wonder weapons reach the front". This picture is not sharp enough to see the model designation, but as the rear sight pedestal has rails for a scope mount, the weapon must be an MP43/1.

Russia, January/February 1944.

(Bundesarchiv Koblenz No. 691/227/12A)

On this picture the soldier opens the small compartment in the butt of the MP43/1. This compartment contained an instruction booklet, the cleaning brush for the gas cilinder, a muzzle cover and the dismantling tool. The dimensions of the compartment also neatly fit the metal oiler of the cleaning device 34, but this was not intended.
Russia, January/February 1944.
(Bundesarchiv Koblenz No. 691/227/9A)

This well-known picture shows a German soldier on the Eastern Front with a reversable windjammer, which was normally worn by mountain or ski troops. Although in other publications his weapon has been described as a *Sturmgewehr* 44, the unstepped barrel and the front sight pedestal clearly define it as an MP43/1. Also note the rail for a telescopic sight on the rear sight pedestal. Russia, 1943/1944.
(Bundesarchiv Koblenz No. 101/90/3938/36)

"The reconnaissence patrol of a cavalry unit has gotten nearer to its target and taken an anticipating firing position", the original caption reads. The men are well-clad in winter uniforms, gloves, felt snow boots and fur caps, and all are armed with a *Sturmgewehr* or one of its predecessors. At the time this picture was taken (January, 1945) such well-equipped troops had become a rare sight.

Place unknown, January 16, 1945.

(Museum of Modern History, Slovenia No. 6487/8)

This series of photos shows Field Marshal Albrecht Kesselring, Commander in Chief in Italy, and an abundance of officers at a demonstration of several types of firearms. On display are an MP43/1, a K98k with rifle grenade launcher, a Gewehr 41, an MP40, an MG34 and an MG42. The date is given as 1944, but strangely enough there is no Gewehr 43 present. The pieces of paper lying on top of the weapons have information about their essentials.
Italy, 1944.
(Bundesarchiv Koblenz No. 580/1980/3)

When the Field Marshal is busy, everyone else is silent, the caption of this picture could read. It is difficult to say what is so special about the clip of 7.9 x 57 mm cartridges that Kesselring is studying, but is does have his full attention. One might be inclined to think it was the first time he ever got to see such a clip. Note that Kesselring carries an interim Marshall staff, intended for daily use.

Italy, 1944.

(Bundesarchiv Koblenz No. 580/1980/4)

With the ejection port cover open, an officer prepares to fire the MP43/1 from the prone position, under the watchfull eye of Kesselring. Appropriate for such important company, a blanket prevents the uniform from getting dirty.
Italy, 1944.
(Bundesarchiv Koblenz No. 580/1980/8)

An officer in a rubber *Kradmantel* takes aim. This coat was officially distributed to motorcyclists only, but was highly appreciated by officers and NCO's of all units as well. Note the shooter holds the MP at the magazine housing and not at the handguard, as he should have done.

Italy, 1944.

(Bundesarchiv Koblenz No. 580/1980/10)

A smiling officer, most likely an *Oberleutnant*, just prior or after firing the MP43/1.
The company apparently quite enjoys the shooting session, as a short moment of relaxation.
The interim Marshall staff of Kesselring is clearly visible here.
Italy, 1944
(Bundesarchiv Koblenz No. 580/1980/13)

An air force pilot takes his turn with the MP43/1 and he prefers to hold the weapon at the magazine housing as well. On his breast he carries the *Flugzeugführer* (pilot) badge and a *Frontflugspanne*, indicating combat experience at the front. On the original picture the fire selector button clearly sticks out to the right, indicating the weapon fires automatic.
Italy, 1944
(Bundesarchiv Koblenz No. 580/1980/11)

A well-clad group of soldiers on the Russian front. As this martial picture shows, the Germans were quite eager to use Soviet sub-machine guns, such as this PPD 1940 with its 71-round drum magazine. By the time this picture was taken, in early 1942, captured Soviet weapons such as these were the only means to increase German fire power. It would not be until a full year later the first MKb's reached the front. Russia, early 1942. (Bundesarchiv Koblenz No. 4/3644/21)

The original caption of this picture reads: """You've been lucky", says Knight's Cross-bearer SS-Hauptscharführer Schreiber, looking at the self-loading rifle of a wounded comrade, whom he encountered during the siege of Tscherkassy. An enemy bullet pierced the stock as the SS-Oberscharführer was under cover. The rifle saved his life". The *Oberscharführer*, of the SS-division Westland as shown on his cuff-title, points at the hole in the stock of his Gewehr 41 (W).

Russia, March 22, 1944.

(Museum of Modern History, Slovenia No. 6624/4)

A very pleased young airforce grenadier just received the Iron Cross second class. On his right arm, he carries a *Sonderabzeichen* for the single-handed destruction of an enemy tank, which may explain the presence of the Panzerfaust in this picture. The grenadier is armed with a captured Soviet PPS-43 submachine gun at a time when he should have had an MP43 or 44. Eastern Front, 1944 (Bundesarchiv Koblenz No. 463/366A/2)

During the Russian campaign, the Germans captured vast quantities of weapons and equipment, a lot of which was used against its former owners. In this picture, a Soviet soldier stockpiles Mosin-Nagant rifles and ammunition pouches. Unfortunately, the exact circumstances are unknown.
Russia, date unknown.
(Bundesarchiv Koblenz No. 10/902/14A)

A group of muddy German parachute troops study a captured Thompson M1928A1 submachine gun. Guns such as these, and the vast number of Soviet submachine guns, made a big impression on the Germans. Note the very early Walther P38 (recognisable by the circular depression around the lanyard ring) in the left man's breast pocket. This soldier has a camouflaged smock, called the *Knochensack* (bone bag) while the man on the far right has a plain green smock.
Tunesia, 1943
(Bundesarchiv Koblenz
No. 788/9/12A)

A prized trophy: a Thompson M1928 submachine gun carried by an *Oberleutnant* of the Africa corps. The caption of this picture has been lost, but the prominent postion of the Swastika flag wrapped around the spare tire of this *Kübelwagen*, makes quite clear what the photographer had in mind.

Northern Africa, 1942.

(Bundesarchiv Koblenz No. 784/226/7)

According to the accompanying information, this series of pictures was taken after the attempt to assassinate Hitler, on July 20, 1944. This suggests that the group of mountain troops had something to do with the hunt for the conspirators. In reality, however, it seems more lilely that these men are receiving basic training. Their wide variety of arms and equipment include an MG42, a K98 with rifle grenade launcher and an MP43 or 44.

State territory, Summer of 1944.

(Bundesarchiv Koblenz No. 676/7996/4A)

The mountain soldier installs the special sight on his K98 with rifle grenaude launcher, while his collegues are buckling up.
Note the MP43 or 44 lying on the ground, its ejection port cover open.
State territory, Summer of 1944.
(Bundesarchiv Koblenz No. 676/7996/3A)

Dressed up in his camouflaged shelter quarter and an improvised camouflage to his field cap, this mountain soldier makes an impressive figure. Strangely enough, however, he carries an MP43 or 44, but has the magazine pouch of an MP40 on his belt, which makes an odd combination. State territory, Summer of 1944. (Bundesarchiv Koblenz No. 676/7996/12)

This close-up of the same soldier makes an impressive silhouet. Here, the strange combination of the MP43 or 44, and the MP40 magazine pouches, clearly shows. Maybe the photographer thought the MP43 or 44 showed better and that no one would note the pouches.
State territory, Summer of 1944.
(Bundesarchiv Koblenz No. 676/7996/13)

An unidentifiable soldier, clad in a reversable windjammer wades through the icy waters of some marshes, getting very cold feet. The butt of the MP is used as a support, showing one of the weak points of the weapon. The main-spring was housed in the butt and when the wood of the butt became swollen, this spring could get squeezed.
Russia, February/March 1944.
(Bundesarchiv Koblenz
No. 693/288/9)

Two soldiers in winter uniforms driving a *Kettenkrad*. Although there is no snow, their weapons still show the traces of winter. Note the white paint on the MP43, and the same on the K98 in the vehicle holder.
Russia, February/March 1944.
(Bundesarchiv Koblenz No. 693/284/12)

The caption to this picture reads: "Rainy days in the puszta. Through weeks of rain the flat puszta has become completely soaked and covered with puddles, so that the vehicles of our armoured division must laboriously find their way through the mudded territory". The picture was made by *Kriegsberichter* Beissel. The radio operator in the SdKfz 251 has his MP43/1 at hand. On his uniform he carries an SA sports badge. Hungary, November 16, 1944. (Museum of Modern History, Slovenia No. 6622/7)

"In places where the mud does not allow the construction of fortifications, German Jäger have taken well-camouflaged battle positions. Here they lay in ambush and many a Soviet reconnaissance unit was scattered", the original caption reads. Both men appear to have an MP43/1 which, at that time and place, was scant comfort.

Eastern front, March 25, 1944.

(Museum of Modern History, Slovenia No. 6487/7)

This picture by SS-*Kriegsberichter* Hoppe shows a rare gun: an MKb 42 (H), equipped with a bayonet lug. Although the photographer did a good job, the picture seems to be posed, as the ejection port cover is closed.

Place and date unknown.

(Bundesarchiv Koblenz No. 146/93/28/14)

Three soldiers during a battle pause. The corporal is about to light his pipe while the man with the MP is adjusting his wrist watch. The K98k features a rifle grenade launcher and the clamp of the special sight is visible on the lower part of the stock. The MP has its safety set, the safety lever being in the upper position. Russia, May/June 1944. (Bundesarchiv Koblenz No. 280/1099/15)

A second lieutenant on the lookout, two stick grenades and an MP43 or 44 at hand. It would not have been very difficult to invent a striking caption for this picture, which is evidently posed: an officer would normally leave this job to one of his men.

Eastern front, Summer of 1944.

(Bundesarchiv Koblenz No. 696/442/31)

A group of mountain
soldiers during a rest. The
men are well-equipped and
the charcteristic silhouet of
the MP43/1 with its unstepped barrel and the square
front sight pedestal is clearly
visible.

The remarkable thing about
this weapon is that it has
two slings, the regular one
and one taken from a K98.
The reason for this is
unknown.

Russia, Spring of 1944.
(Bundesarchiv Koblenz
No. 90/3912/20A)

The pictures on these two pages show a more or less comparable situation, but a different armament. The soldier on this photo has a Russian PPSh 41 submachine gun, with a 71-round drum magazine. In the course of the war, the Germans were using thousands of captured Russians submachine guns, which they wanted to replace with *Maschinenkarabiner*. By the time this picture was taken, however, production of the latter was still getting under way.

Mid-Russia, December 1942.

(Bundesarchiv Koblenz No. 150/1742/35)

This member of the *Gebirgsjäger* (Mountain Troops) is equipped as the Germans had envisaged. As the weapon has the rail for a telescopic sight, it is most likely an MP43/1.

The frequent appearance of this model is remarkable, as the number of MP43/1's was only about 3 percent of the total *Sturmgewehr* production. Mid-Russia, January/February 1944. (Bundesarchiv Koblenz No. 692/262/32A)

A small group of Mountain Troops crosses wooded territory in Mid-Russia. The large amount of small trees made it difficult for the photographer to get a clear picture. The conditions look very cold, yet the soldier holding the MP43/1 does not have gloves. Mid-Russia, January/February 1944.
(Bundesarchiv Koblenz No. 692/262/21A)

In this second view of the same group of Mountain Troops the photographer got a better shot. Note the man up front is carrying two machine gun belt boxes. The *Gebirgsjäger* with the MP43/1 has an old-type magazine pouch closed by one single large flap.

Mid-Russia, January/February 1944.

(Bundesarchiv Koblenz No. 692/262/23A)

An assault engineers group advances through the rubbles of a Belgian town. The soldier in front of the MP43 (or 44) bearer, carries a Model 41 flame-thrower. The rest of the team has K98k rifles and is bent under the load of explosives. Belgium, fall of 1944.
(Leszek Erenfeicht)

A group of new recruits at the training ground hand their brand-new MPs to the senior NCO for the inspection. The young soldier failed to remove the web carrying sling, and now has to stand close to his superior, clutching the butt, the main spring and the bolt carrier with its long piston.
Place unknown, October 23, 1944.
(Leszek Erenfeicht)

Mountain Troops crossing a stream. The men carry the reversable wind jammer and large backpacks, which were originally only intented for troops in the high mountains. The front man has the old-type magazine pouch with one single flap, which evidently gave insufficient protection as one magazine is clearly visible. Mid-Russia, January/February 1944.
(Bundesarchiv Koblenz No. 692/263/36)

An *Oberleutnant* (first lieutenant) of ski troops, recognizable by the ranking badge on his left arm, adresses his men. All are armed with MP's, although the exact model is not recognizable. The magazine pouches are of the old model with one single closing flap, and seem to be of different material.
Mid-Russia, January/February 1944.
(Bundesarchiv Koblenz No. 691/245/13A)

In October, 1943, the Infantry School at Döberitz conducted a series of trials with a scoped MP43/1, in comparison with a G43. The scope used was the recently developed ZF4, which was fitted on a mounting rail on the left side of the receiver as shown in this picture of the trials. The MP43/1 proved not suited for the role of a sniper weapon. Döberitz, 1943.

(Militärarchiv Freiburg)

A G43 fitted with a ZF4, during the October 1943 trials at the Infantry School. Mass production of the G43 had by that time only just begun. Although the G43 performed better than the MP43/1, it lacked the qualities of the K98 as a sniper weapon. Up to the end of the war, the Germans kept trying to improve the rifle, with only limited succes. In fact, only some ten percent of all G43s ever got a telescopic sight.

Döberitz, 1943.

(Militärarchiv Freiburg)

A clear picture of the Infantry School trials. The trials report describes the weapon used as an MP43/1, with serial number 918. This gun must have been something of a hybrid, as it has the stepped barrel and redesigned front sight pedestal of the MP43, and shows an unusual muzzle nut.
Döberitz, 1943.
(Militärarchiv Freiburg)

A front view of the MP43/1 with ZF4 scope. This picture clearly shows what many thought one of the main drawbacks of the MP: through its long magazine, it was difficult to take cover and the shooter formed a distinctive silhouette. This complaint, however, was rarely heard from the troops who took this small inconvenience for granted.
Döberitz, 1943.
(Militärarchiv Freiburg)

Another front view of the MP43/1 with ZF4 scope, taken during the Infantry School trials in October, 1943. During these trials, the weapon performed rather poorly. After firing thirty shots fully automatic, the optics were completely dislocated. Efforts to correct the drawbacks were unsuccesfull and by late 1944, all attempts to create a sniper MP were halted.

Döberitz, 1943.

(Militärarchiv Freiburg)

In comparison with the previous page, this picture shows the best sniper weapon the Germans had throughout the war: the good old K98k. Neither the MP's nor the G43 could beat the accuracy of this bolt-action rifle.
Location unknown, May 16, 1944. (Museum of Modern History, Slovenia No. 6619/5)

This very rare picture is the only known example of *Sturmgewehr* manufacture. The original caption reads:

"Ever newer and better weapons. In the past this factory made high quality hunting and sporting arms. Nowadays the production consists of weapons for our fighting front, which are constantly manufactured in tireless labour to equip our troops". Although the caption gives no location, this description quite nicely fits the Haenel factory. The picture was taken by photographer Kompe. Suhl, January 2, 1945. (Museum of Modern History, Slovenia No. 6604/2)

A Mauser factory picture of a *Schießmaschine*, to test MP's, including a device to collect the ejected cartridge cases. The picture is dated November, 1944. A left side view, not pictured here, shows the weapon to be marked "MP44", a designation which was introduced in April.

Oberndorf, 1944.

(H.L. Visser)

These pictures show two Germans in the snow, both armed with an MP43/1. Their camouflage clothing obscures every sign of rank and as the original caption is lost, there is very little left to say. Although the muzzle of the weapon in the foreground is obscured by some bushes, it seems to have a square front sight pedestal, making it an MP43/1.
Russia, late 1943.
(Bundesarchiv Koblenz No. 89/3797/25A)

The two soldiers confer about their further action. Although they are well-clad, their headgear consist of the simple overseas cap, which did not offer much protection from the cold. The better look on the left gun identifies it as an MP43/1.

Russia, late 1943.

(Bundesarchiv Koblenz No. 89/3797/16A)

A grenadier demonstrates to the photographer how to field-strip an MP43/1. The spring-held pin has been pushed out to the right side, thus making it possible to remove the butt. The lower part of the photo is blurred and the grenadier does not look into the camera, so its is very unlikely this picture was ever published. Mid-Russia, January/February 1944.
(Bundesarchiv Koblenz No. 691/227/21)

This time, the photographer did a better job. The grenadier looks into the camera and the light is better. The soldier carries the pants of a winter uniform and has the ribbons of both the Iron Cross second class and the *Ostmedaille* on his tunic. The caption would have said something about the complete confidence of the Germans in their new weapon, emphasized by smoking a pipe. Mid-Russia, January/February 1944.
(Bundesarchiv Koblenz No. 691/227/19A)

Yet another picture of the disassembled MP, trying to find a different composition. The MP43/1 seems to be brand new, as neither the metal nor the sling and butt show any signs of wear. The square front sight pedestal of this model is clearly visible.

Mid-Russia, January/February 1944.

(Bundesarchiv Koblenz No. 691/244/9)

A German soldier struggling through the Russian mud. The weather conditions must have been very bad at the time, for the ground is soft while at the same time it is snowing. Rank, unit and the exact type of MP that this man is carrying, are unidentifiable. Russia, Janaury/February 1944. (Bundesarchiv Koblenz No. 691/244/9)

A group of German soldiers, somewhere in Russia. The time is given as the Spring of 1944, but the weather is still very cold. All men carry winter uniforms and some have painted their helmets white as well. The soldier on the left is one of the lucky few to carry an MP43 or 44.

Russia, Spring of 1944.

(Bundesarchiv Koblenz No. 90/3904/23)

The same group of soldiers, showing their wide variety of equipment. The officer on the left has his MP43/1 set on safe. Note that the machine gun helper on the right has extra clips of cartridges stuck on the outside of his K98 pouches, were they are secured by the straps. This way, unfastening the straps gave immediate access to a new clip, instead of having to open the flaps first.

Russia, Spring of 1944.

(Bundesarchiv Koblenz No. 90/3904/27)

This third picture of the group of soldiers shows their variety of small arms: Two MP43s or 44s, an MP40, an MG42 and some K98s. Such a combination was an impressive amount of firepower, but at the same time these weapons fired three different types of cartridges which may have caused logistic problems.

Russia, Spring of 1944.

(Bundesarchiv Koblenz No. 90/3904/26)

"*Bahnbrecher der Division - Sturmfüseliere in den Karpatenvorbergen*" (Trailblazers of the division - assault fusiliers in the Carpatian headlands), the original caption to this picture reads. Although barely visible, the man in the foreground has an K43 semi-automatic rifle, while his colleague in the middle carries an MP43 or 44. November 25, 1944. (Museum of Modern History, Slovenia No. 6491/10)

This series of pictures was taken by the same photographer as those on pages 114, 115 and 116 and again show a succesfull attempt to portray the MP43/1 in the most impressive way. This first picture clearly shows the distinctive silhouet of the weapon, which seems to be brand new.
Mid-Russia, January/February 1944.
(Bundesarchiv Koblenz No. 691/227/4A)

This second picture, taken somewhat more from the side, clearly shows the main features of the MP43/1: the unstepped barrel, the square front sight pedestal and the rails for a scope mount on the rear sight pedestal. Had the soldier cocked his weapon, the ejection port cover would be open.

Mid-Russia, January/February 1944.

(Bundesarchiv Koblenz No. 691/227/5A)

Viewed from this different angle, the MP43/1 remains an impressive weapon. The sling is loosened a bit, to give a better view of the receiver. It would not be very difficult to write a striking caption.
Mid-Russia, January/February 1944.
(Bundesarchiv Koblenz No. 691/226/29)

This least impressive picture of the series still gives a clear view on the features of the MP43/1. Although the rails for a ZF41 scope mount are present on all weapons of this model, such a scope was never issued. Trials showed that the MP was not suited for the role as a sniper weapon.

Mid-Russia, January/February 1944.

(Bundesarchiv Koblenz No. 691/226/24A)

"A look in no man's land. Well camouflaged and careful, a soldier looks into the wide valley of the mountaineous region between the Eifel and the Bulge. The valley itself is no man's land", the caption says. The picture, by photographer Elle, was taken in the final stages of the Battle of the Bulge, the last major German offensive of the war.
Western part of Germany, January 27, 1945
(Museum of Modern History, Slovenia No. unknown)

This picture by SS-photographer Pospesch shows group of SS-men waiting to receive their battle orders. No weapons are visible, but the picture does clearly show the new type of *Sturmgewehr* magazine pouch, in which each magazine compartment in closed by a separate flap.

Netherlands, November 1944

(Museum of Modern History, Slovenia No. unknown)

What appear to be a sniper and an MP43 or 44 firing at a target in the distance, is in fact a very posed picture, as the sniper carries a whitened tool kit of a machine gun helper as well, a very unlikely combination of tasks. The type of tank is difficult to determine, but seems to be a Tiger I.

Place and date unknown.

(Bundesarchiv Koblenz No. 146/97/74/27)

This picture was apparently made to introduce a new type of weapon in the press: the MP43/1. Regrettably the picture is somewhat obscure, or else it might even have been possible to read the serial number. One of the greater mysteries of the MP43/1 is that although some 14,000 were made, no magazines are known with that designation. Mid-Russia, January/February 1944.
(Bundesarchiv Koblenz No. 691/227/21A)

An Infantry unit in Russia, during a short break. Note the practical manner in which the weapons are put in the snow, effectively preventing snow entering the mechanism. The second soldier from the left has an old model magazine pouch with one single flap.

Northern Russia, September 1943.

(Bundesarchiv Koblenz No. 700/288/24A)

This and the next two pictures show a ski patrol in Russia. This group is well-clad and well-equipped, as all men carry an MP43/1. That, however, is all the good news they had, since in early 1944 the Soviets were rapidly driving back their invaders.

Mid-Russia, January/February 1944.

(Bundesarchiv Koblenz No. 691/245/14A)

Two soldiers of the ski group have taken up firing positions. If this picture was posed, it is a convincing pose, as the man in front has cocked his MP43/1, thereby ejecting a live round that was already in the chamber and now is lying near the stick grenade. The ejection port cover is open, giving a clear view of the mechanism. Mid-Russia, January/February 1944. (Bundesarchiv Koblenz No. 691/245/30A)

The photographer has taken a different postion while the soldier is gesturing at his comrades. The live round that has been ejcted by cocking the MP43/1 is clearly visible in the snow.

Mid-Russia, January/February 1944.

(Bundesarchiv Koblenz No. 691/245/27A)

A cigarette break for German cavalrymen. From their riding boots and breeches these men look like a regular cavalry unit. Note the different styles of carrying the MP. The NCO carries his muzzle up, with no magazine, while the soldier he gives light to carries his muzzle down and has the magazine inserted.
Russia, July 1944
(Leszek Erenfeicht)

An Infantry unit on the lookout in mid-Russia. All three visible weapons are MP43/1's, the only variety of the MP that had been produced in quantity by early 1944. The weapons are easily recognisable by their square front sight pedestal. All three have rails for a telescopic sight.

Russia, March 1944.

(Bundesarchiv Koblenz No. 693/287/11)

A group of Infantrymen in a posed "combat" shot. They are camouflaged to their teeth, but clearly wearing the assault badges and carefully exposing the NCO *Tresse*, or silver bands around their uniform jacket collars. They carry the latest in Infantry armament, including an MP43 or 44, an MG42 and a Panzerfaust. Plaze and date unknown (Leszek Erenfeicht)

Riding the King Tiger, these parachutists can rest their feet for a while. Impressive a weapon as the Sturmgewehr was, its silhouet is nothing compared to the tank gun.

Place and date unknown.

(Leszek Erenfeicht)

Two soldiers are walking
through a deserted and
ruined city, mauled so much
that any identification
points are obliterated.
No original caption has
survived, so it is impossible
to say whether this town is
in the East or West.
Place and date unknown
(Leszek Erenfeicht)

By the time this picture was taken, in late 1944, large parts of the German army had become "de-motorised", so apart from the latest in small arms, the MP44, these men were issued the trusted friend of an armed man – a horse. The picture is dated November 6, 1944, but this is obviously impossible, judging from the foliage.
Russia, 1944
(Leszek Erenfeicht)

Two German soldiers on the lookout in which is very obviously a posed picture, as the MG42 has no cartridge belt.
The MP43/1 has a double sling. Although the weapon is carried over the schoulder, a second sling is hanging downward.
The magazine pouch is of the old type with a single closing flap. Mid-Russia, January/February 1944.
(Bundesarchiv Koblenz No. 691/244/11)

"The men of a reconaissance unit, who just faced difficult and dangerous moments while stalking out enemy positions on the opposite side, take a breather below dense thicket", the original caption reads. Although their winter camouflage makes identification impossible, the picture was taken by SS-photographer Rottensteiner, so it may be assumed that this is an SS-unit. The men are heavily armed, with an MG42, a K43 on the right, and a *Sturmgewehr*.

Place unknown, January 24, 1945.

(Museum of Modern History, Slovenia No. unknown)

A German soldier urges his comrades to the advance, with the menacing silhouet of a burning half-track in the background. The rather cheerfull expression on his face leads to believe this picture was posed. The sheet metal handguard of an MP is just visible, but the exact model is impossible to determine.
Belgium, December 1944
(Leszek Erenfeicht)

Weary and grim, young Waffen-SS Estonian volunteers trudge along a muddy path. The place is the Kurland Peninsula, and the date the Fall of 1944. They have nothing to smile about, as they are cut off, defending their own country against the Soviets and they know they are going to lose. The soldier with the MP helps his mate, an MG-team ammunition bearer, to carry his burden.

Kurland Peninsula, Fall of 1944.

(Leszek Erenfeicht)

In the last months of the war, it became increasingly difficult to write inspiring captions, so here it simply says: "SS-paratroopers fight on the Oder. The head of a motorized storm troop gets under fire". The situation, however, seems a little too relaxed for this to be true.

The most noteworthy of this picture is the fact that the man on the right carries an MKb 42 (H). Whether these trials weapons were re-issued late in the war or whether this particular specimen had survived almost three years of fighting is unknown.

Eastern Front, February 1945.

(Museum of Modern History, Slovenia No. 6004/7)

This picture of rather poor quality shows a group of German soldiers on the march through muddy terrain. The leader carries an MP of unknown model. The men show nothing of the victorious mood they had three years earlier, marching in the opposite direction.

Mid-Russia, January/February 1944.

(Bundesarchiv Koblenz No. 690/224/29)

Guerrilla fighters everywhere used whatever weapons they could lay their hands on. Here, the two Polish resistance fighters pose proudly with their captured MPs. The weapon on the left lacks the handguard. Note the remarkable afro hairstyle of the man on the left which, had he been a regular soldier, would have brought him trouble with any NCO in the world.

Poland, date unknown
(Leszek Erenfeicht)

Another group of Polish resistance fighters, armed in a colourful way: two *Sturmgewehre* on the left, a Beretta M38A, an MG34 and the commander's Soviet PPSh M1941. This photo of a Home Army unit, partly wearing Polish prewar uniforms, was taken in the then Polish part of what is now Lithuania. These troops tried to re-organise Polish administration and were first aided by the Soviets, but later arrested by NKVD security troops and deported to Siberia forced labour camps, and released only in the mid-1950s.

Nowogrodek, date unknown.

(Leszek Erenfeicht)

"From cover to cover the storm troop works its way towards the enemy", the caption says. In January, 1945, when photographer Scheck took this picture, there was little more to say, although these soldiers are still reasonably well equipped, with a Model 41 flame-thrower and a *Sturmgewehr*.

Place unknown, January 15, 1945.

(Museum of Modern History, Slovenia No. 6604/1)

In the last stages of the war, many civilians were summoned to defend the remains of the Third Reich. The military situation for Germany was hopeless, but the Nazi's continued to sacrifice thousands of lives. Only a fraction of the millions of *Sturmgewehre* anticipated had been produced, and so these men carry a wide variety of arms, most notably a Haenel-made MP41 in the centre.

Germany, January 25, 1945.

(Museum of Modern History, Slovenia No. 6605/11)

A picture that tells a thousands words. Children play amidst a variety of weapons and equipment in April, 1945. The weapons have been rendered useless by removing the stocks, which indeed was one of the principal weaknesses of the *Sturmgewehr*. The main spring was housed within the wooden stock, vulnerable at the joint with the receiver. Should the stock break of, the weapon became useless.

Germany, April 1945.

(Leszek Erenfeicht)

X SOURCES, LITERATURE & NOTES

Sources

The information on which this book is based, stems mainly from original sources. The most important documents are kept in the *Bundesarchiv Militärarchiv* (German Military Archives) at Freiburg. Where appropriate, they are cited below.

Although the archives answer most questions, some literature has been used. The most important book on the Sturmgewehr is *Vom Gewehr 98 zum Sturmgewehr*, by Hans-Dieter Handrich which, regrettably, has found only limited attention. Through this book in fact, we learned about the existence of the archives in Freiburg. Other books and articles that were used are listed below.

Literature

– H.D. Götz, *German Military Rifles and Machine Pistols 1871-1945* (West Chester 1990)

– H.-D. Handrich, *Vom Gewehr 98 zum Sturmgewehr* (Bonn 1993)

– O.-H. von Lossnitzer, *Das Deutsche Sturmgewehr* (typescript, 1947).

– P. Senich, *Deutsche Sturmgewehre bis 1945* (Stuttgart 1998)

– "Das Sturmgewehr 44 seine Vorläufer und Varianten", *Waffen Revue* 43, 6795-6842.

Notes

1. On October 16, 1944, the General der Infanterie beim Chef Generalstabs des Heeres sent a suggestion by General Jaschka for a different designation, to propose to Hitler. Bundesarchiv, Militärarchiv Freiburg RH 11/1/54.

2. Sitzung der Inspektion für Waffen und Gerät und des Reichswehrministeriums über das Zukunfts-l.M.G. am 6.6.21, in: Militärarchiv Freiburg, RH 12/2/149.

3. "Das Sturmgewehr 44 seine Vorläufer und Varianten", *Waffen Revue* 43, 6796.

4. Report Infantry School from June 30, 1942, in: Militärarchiv Freiburg, RH 11/1/52.

5. Denkschrift über einen Maschinenkarabiner, Chef Heeres Rüstung und BdE, WaA Az. 72 b 0012/4 Wa Prüf 2 I 6 Bd. Nr. 03369/42 g, November 18, 1942, in: Militärarchiv Freiburg, RH 11/1/53.

6. Erfahrungsbericht zum Vergleichsschiessen zwischen Karabiner 98 k und Maschinenkarabiner 42, December 3, 1942, in: Militärarchiv Freiburg, RH 12/2/139.

7. Telegram General Stab des Heeres/Organisations Abteilung, Chef Heeres Rüstung und Bekleidung to OKW/Heeresstab, February 7, 1943, in: Militärarchiv Freiburg, RH 11/1/52.

8. General der Infanterie beim Oberkommando des Heeres to Heeresgruppe Nord, April 10, 1943, in: Militärarchiv Freiburg, RH 11/1/52.

9. Memorandum of October 2, 1943, in: Militärarchiv Freiburg, RH 11/1/52.

10. "Vorschlag fur die Durchführung eines Infanterie-Programms" from Oberstleutnant d.G. Inhofer,

Heereswaffenamt, Stab Ia, Berlijn, November 10, 1943, in: Militärarchiv Freiburg, RH 11/1/50.

11. OKH to all parties, February 14, 1944, in: Militärarchiv Freiburg, RH 11/1/52.

12. General Stab des Heeres to all parties, April 25, 1944, in: Militärarchiv Freiburg, RH 11/1/52.

13. Anlage 3 zu OKH/General Stab des Heeres/ Organisations Abteilung Nr. I 17, June 16, 1944, in: Militärarchiv Freiburg RH 12/2/138.

14. Aktennotiz über die Besprechung bei der Fa. C.G. Haenel, Suhl, December 1, 1943, in: Militärarchiv Freiburg, RH 12/2/139.

15. Erfahrungsbericht der Infanterie Schule Grafenwöhr, March 23, 1945, in: Militärarchiv Freiburg, RH 12/2/139.

16. Bericht über die Sitzung der Sonderkommission Infanteriewaffen in Döbeln am 29. und 30.8.1944, in: Militärarchiv Freiburg RH 12/2/126.

17. O.-H. von Lossnitzer, *Das Deutsche Sturmgewehr* (typescript, 1947).

18. WaA to Reichsminister für Rüstung und Kriegs- produktion, June 27, 1944, in: Militärarchiv Freiburg, RH 12/2/139.

19. Bericht über die Sitzung der Sonderkommission Infanteriewaffen in Döbeln am 29. und 30.8.1944, in: Militärarchiv Freiburg RH 12/2/130.

20. P. Senich, *Deutsche Sturmgewehre bis 1945* (Stuttgart 1998), 142.

21. Report Infantry School, October 22, 1943, in: Militärarchiv Freiburg, RH 11/1/52.

22. Rheinmetall-Borsig Bericht Nr. 1446, in: Militärarchiv Freiburg, RH 11/1/54.

23 Aktenvermerk zur Besprechung über "Krummer Lauf" bei Fa. Rheinmetall/Borsig in Unterlüss am 24 10.1944, in: Militärarchiv Freiburg, RH 12/2/139.

24. Aktenvermerk über die Besprechung bei Wa Prüf 2 I e am 8.12.1944, in: Militärarchiv Freiburg, RH 12/ 2/140.

25. General der Infanterie, Notiz über Waffenvorführung am 13.9.44 in Kummersdorf, in: Militärarchiv Freiburg, RH 11/1/46.

26. C.G. Haenel, Verzeichnis unserer Unterlieferanten für STg 44 mit Angaben der von diesen Firmen gefertigten Teilen, in: Thüringisches Staatsarchiv Meiningen, C.G. Haenel Archive.